橘　由加 監修・編著
Linc Educational Resources, Inc 編

オンライン英語学習用テキスト

lincEnglish
Bronze II

大学教育出版

はじめに

　本書は Linc Educational Resources, Inc. が開発した、総合的英語力を伸ばすオンライン学習システム Linc English の Bronze II（レベル表参照）のコンテンツをテキスト用に編集したものです。Linc English はリスニング、リーディング、文法・語彙、ライティングの総合的英語能力をのばすためのオンライン英語学習教材です。また、英検および TOEFL、TOEIC、センター試験のスコア・アップのために、聴解、読解、文法・語彙、筆記の能力養成教材としても有効です。この総合英語カリキュラムで学習することにより、ハイレベルな英語力の向上を狙います。留学準備、大学や大学院入学対策にもなります。カリキュラムは中1年生（英検5級程度）から上級までのレベルで構成されており、多量のコンテンツを学習することにより、総合的な英語力を身につけることを目標としています。

　日本人の英語学習者に不足しているのは、①英語を聞き続ける「持久力」、②英語で即反応できる「瞬発力」の2つの力です。また学習量、学習時間が不足しているため、読解力、聴解力の弱さが目立ちます。学校の現場では、①教科書だけで徹底的に鍛えることが難しい、②多量の宿題を出しても、採点する時間がない、③授業以外で十分な時間をとることが難しい、などが現状ではないでしょうか。このような問題を解決するためには、授業＋セルフスタディーの学習リズムを作る必要があります。そこで開発されたのが Linc English です。本書 Bronze II は、TOEIC：200〜300、TOEFL（PBT）：350〜400、（CBT）：63〜97、英検3級レベル、準2級レベルの学習者を対象としています。

　Linc English のコンセプトデザインは、①カリキュラム・ティーム、②システム、③コンテンツの3つから成り立っています。学習するコンテンツはすべて、現役のアメリカ人コラムニストや ESL の専門家が日本人のために作成した完全オリジナルです。音声は、リスニング問題はもちろん、リーディング問題にも収録されています。インターネットを活用するので、学校でも家でも学習することができ、学習者は都合に合わせて演習に取り組むことができます。採点は自動的に行われるので、教師の採点作業が一切不要になります。学習時間、到達度、評価などをパソコンで把握できます（自動採点システム、学習管理機能システム搭載）。膨大なコンテンツ量で、年間24レッスンをカリキュラムとした場合、演習時間をテキストに書き出すと A4 判にしておよそ 2,500 ページにもなりますが、コンテンツの量や難易度を調整し、アップデートをしていくことができます。

　Linc English オンライン・カリキュラムはトータルで216レッスン、28,000以上の演習問題、A4判で18,000ページにもおよぶ莫大なコンテンツ量です。レベルは Pre Bronze（I, II）、Bronze（I, II, III）、Silver（I, II, III）Gold（I, II, III）、Platinum A（I, II, III）、Platinum B（I, II, III）から構成されています。Linc English は個人別・能力別に学習者のレベルに合わせ、自分のペースで学習を進めることができます。リスニング、リーディング教材のトピックはショート・ストーリー、エッセイ、文芸、芸術、歴史、異文化、政治・経済、世界情勢、ニュース、情報、環境、スポーツ、哲学、論説文など多岐にわたっています。教材はやさしい段階から少しず

つ高度な内容へと6レベル、17セクション構成になっています。

　自分のペースで何回でも演習できるので、確実に英語力をのばしたい学習者にとっては、絶対必須のカリキュラムです。またオンライン上で学習管理が容易にできるので、英語力がどのように上達しているか把握できます。英語力をつけるには毎日数時間の集中学習が必要です。語学学習は演習量がものをいいます。興味深いコンテンツで膨大な演習問題をこなしていく、そんな学習法が英語教育では必要ではないでしょうか。

　学校の先生方にはLinc Englishを是非CALL授業でお使いになることをお勧めします。英語のカリキュラムの一環として授業と連動させながら、補足教材としてLinc Englishで指導することもできるでしょう。コンテンツを本書のようにテキスト化した理由は、教師・学習者がコンピュータルーム以外でも、一般の英語の授業で使えるようにするためです。また自宅にインターネット環境のパソコンがない場合は、学校でパソコンで演習し、自宅ではテキストで学習できます。授業でLinc Englishをお使いになる場合の授業プラン、指導案も「本書の構成と活用法」で簡単に説明いたしますので、参考にしていただければ幸いです。CALL授業のカリキュラムに何かのプログラムをすでに導入されている場合は、学習者個人の自主学習教材として利用していただくこともできます。アメリカの大学留学のためのTOEFL対策、就職準備や英語力向上のため、TOEICのスコアを上げたい学習者にとって、Linc Englishは最適なオンライン学習教材です。

　最後になりますが、問題作成に協力していただいたLinc Englishカリキュラム・ティームの皆様に感謝の意を表したいと思います。なお、本書の製作にあたっては、大学教育出版代表の佐藤守氏、および三好弘明氏から多大な協力を頂きました。末筆になりましたが、この場を借りて改めてお礼を申し上げます。

2009年2月

監修者・編著者　橘　由加

本書の構成と効果的な活用法

　本書は12レッスンからなり、各レッスンは7種のプラクティス演習で構成されています。これを〈Part〉とよびます。本書は、Linc Englishのデジタルコンテンツの演習問題と解説をテキスト用に編集してまとめたものです。学習者の自宅学習のテキストとして、また学校の授業でも使えるように配慮しています。以下にカリキュラム概要、オンライン教材と本書を併用した授業プラン（指導案）を説明します。

Linc Englishカリキュラムの概要

* 学生、高校生、大学生、社会人を対象とした総合英語学習カリキュラムです。
* 英語の4技能（リスニング、リーディング、ライティング、スピーキング）の発達を目指します。
* 英検、TOEIC、TOEFLの対策や受験英語、ビジネス英語、英語教員養成英語など、さまざまな用途別のオンライン英語学習とも連結しています。
* レベルは全部で6レベル。やさしい内容から少しずつ高度な内容へと17セクションの構成になっており、個人別・能力別に学習者のレベルに合わせ、自分のペースで学習することができます。
* リスニングやリーディング教材のトピックは、エッセイ、芸術、文芸、政治・経済、世界情勢など多岐にわたっています。
* 授業プランや指導用のマニュアルも用意しており、通常の対面型授業を補完する学習システムとして利用できます。またレベルごとのテキストブックも揃えており、他のオンライン学習システムと大きく異なるところです。

教材のレベルと学習対象者

　Linc Englishは、Pre Bronze（Ⅰ, Ⅱ）、Bronze（Ⅰ, Ⅱ, Ⅲ）、Silver（Ⅰ, Ⅱ, Ⅲ）、Gold（Ⅰ, Ⅱ, Ⅲ）、Platinum A（Ⅰ, Ⅱ, Ⅲ）、Platinum B（Ⅰ, Ⅱ, Ⅲ）、の全部で6レベルから構成され、17セクションに分かれています。中学1年生から英語教育者・上級レベルの社会人まで、豊富なラインアップとなっています。中学生の場合は1年間の授業で18レッスン、高校生から大学生の場合は1年間で24レッスンで終了できるような指導をお勧めします。

17 Levels & Standards	Grade	Score
Pre Bronze Ⅰ, Ⅱ	中学生（初級・低）	TOEIC: 50〜150（TOEICブリッジ: 20〜180）／TOEFL: PBT 300〜350　CBT 20〜63／英検：5級・4級
Bronze Ⅰ, Ⅱ, Ⅲ	中学3年生・高校生（初級・高）	TOEIC: 200〜300／TOEFL: PBT 350〜400　CBT 63〜97／英検：3級・準2級
Silver Ⅰ, Ⅱ, Ⅲ	高校3年生・大学生（中級・低）	TOEIC: 300〜450／TOEFL: PBT 400〜460　CBT 97〜140／英検：準2級・2級
Gold Ⅰ, Ⅱ, Ⅲ	大学生（中級・高）	TOEIC: 450〜600／TOEFL: PBT 460〜500　CBT 140〜173／英検：2級・準1級
Platinum A Ⅰ, Ⅱ, Ⅲ	大学生・一般・ビジネスマン（上級）	TOEIC: 600〜800／TOEFL: PBT 500〜570　CBT 173〜230／英検：準1級
Platinum B Ⅰ, Ⅱ, Ⅲ	大学生・英語教育者（上級）	TOEIC: 800〜990／TOEFL: PBT 570〜677　CBT 173〜300／英検：1級

* レベルと対象学習者はあくまでも目安です。学習者の能力や必要に応じて、レベルを選べます。
* 児童、小学生、児童英語教育関係者対象のLinc Kids Englishもございます。

Linc Englishオンライン・カリキュラム（レッスンの構造）

種別	内容	問題数
リスニング	写真描写問題	25問
	質疑応答問題	30問
	会話問題	30問
	説明文問題	10問
リーディング	段落速読問題	12問
	読解問題	4問
	文脈問題	3問
グラマー&ボキャブラリー	空所補充問題	40問
	誤文訂正問題	25問
レッスン合計		179問

※Bronze〜Goldの例

Linc Englishテキスト構成

- PartⅠ　Image Listening／写真描写問題
- PartⅡ　Question and Response／質疑応答問題
- PartⅢ　Short Conversation／会話問題
- PartⅣ　Short Talks／説明文問題
- PartⅤ　Reading／読解問題
- PartⅥ　Error Recognition／空所補充問題
- PartⅦ　Incomplete Sentence／文法・語彙問題

＊　テキストには、リーディング・セクションの段落速読問題と文脈問題は掲載していません。
＊　問題も抜粋して、順序を変えています。

オンラインでの演習所要時間の目安

　各レベルの演習所要時間はあくまで目安です。セルフ・スタディーでは、1レッスンを1週間かけて終了するつもりで、何回も演習を繰り返してください。毎日最低でも1時間以上の学習を目標にすると、英語力がついてきます。先生方には学校でLinc Englishを導入して授業で利用する場合、各レッスンを2週間かけて終了することをお勧めします。またテキストを使って自宅学習、筆記の宿題も出すことができます。授業用に20分ほどのクイズも用意していますので、最初の1週目の授業でレッスンのポイントや演習のコツを学ばせ、2週目の授業でクイズをし、答え合わせや解説を行うなど、いろいろと工夫のある授業が考えられます。

　＊以下に記す授業の進め方、授業モデルを参照

（1）中学生対象：プリ・ブロンズのオンライン演習とテキスト構成

　プリ・ブロンズは、各レッスン6種のプラクティス（演習）から構成されており、テキストではプラクティスを6種（part）としています。テキストはオンライン演習と同じ内容ですが、教材の一部の演習問題と解説を編集してテキスト用にまとめています。

●リスニング・セクション：4種のプラクティス（テキストではPart）
　1．写真描写問題　　15問　（時間約8分）
　2．質疑応答問題　　20問　（10分）

3．会話問題　　　　　15問　（8分）
　4．説明文問題　　　　10問　（12分）
● リーディングセクション： 1種のプラクティス
　5．読解問題　　　　　4〜5段落　5問　（時間約10分）
● 文法・語彙セクション：1種のプラクティス
　6．空所補充問題　　　25問　（時間15分）

＊各レッスンを約60分で終了させることを目標とする

（2）　高校・大学生対象：ブロンズ〜ゴールドのオンライン演習とテキスト構成

　ブロンズ〜ゴールドは、各レッスン9種のプラクティス（演習）から構成されていますが、テキストではプラクティスを7種（Part）としています。テキストはオンライン演習と同じ内容ですが、教材の一部の演習問題と解説を編集してテキスト用にまとめています。

● リスニングセクション：4種のプラクティス（テキストではPart）
　1．描写問題　　　　　25問　（時間約12分）
　2．質疑応答問題　　　30問　（時間約12分）
　3．会話問題　　　　　30問　（時間約12分）
　4．説明文問題　　　　10問　（時間約12分）
● リーディングセクション：　3種のプラクティスであるが段落問題と読解問題の本文は同じ内容
　5．段落速読問題（時間制限有り）　4段落　12問　（時間約7分）　テキストには載せていない
　6．読解問題　　　　　4段落　　　　4問　（時間約10分）
　7．文脈問題　　　　　2〜3段落　　3問　（時間約6分）　テキストには載せていない
● 文法・語彙セクション：2種のプラクティス
　1．空所補充問題　　　40問　（時間約20分）
　2．誤文訂正問題　　　25問　（時間約12分）

＊各レッスンを約100分で終了させることを目標とする

（3）　大学生・社会人対象：プラチナのオンライン演習教材とテキスト構成

　プラチナは、各レッスン6種のプラクティス（演習）から構成されていますが、テキストではプラクティスを5種（Part）としています。テキストはオンライン演習と同じ内容ですが、教材の一部の演習問題と解説を編集してテキスト用にまとめています。

● リスニンググセクション：1種のプラクティス（テキストではPart）
　1．説明文問題　　　　10問　（時間約12〜15分）
● リーディングセクション：3種のプラクティス
　2．段落速読問題　（時間制限有り）　4段落　12問　（時間約　7分）　テキストには載せていない
　3．読解問題　　　　　4段落　　　　4問　（時間約15分）
　4．文脈問題　　　　　2〜3段落　　3問　（時間約7分）　テキストには載せていない
● 文法・語彙セクション：2種のプラクティス
　5．空所補充問題題　　20問　（10分）
　6．誤文訂正問題　　　12問　（8分）

＊各レッスンを約60分で終了させることを目標とする

本書（Bronze Ⅱ）を併用したLinc English授業モデル＜高校生レベル＞

英語の授業を円滑に進めるためには、最低限度の英語運用能力、「読む、書く、聞く、話す」という4技能と「文法、発音、語彙」の3領域の充実が求められますが、特に文法、語彙という形式操作能力とリーディング、リスニングという受容能力（インプット）の訓練が強く求められます。よく「会話力」の向上を求める声が高まっていますが、リスニングと文法・語彙を確実にすることで、初めてコミュニケーション能力が育成されます。このようなことから、学習者個人の能力に合わせた最適な環境、いわゆる自主学習を通して基礎力の補強を支援するCALL教育が必要となります。CALLは、本来個別学習を特色としますが、教室内外で学習者が自分のペースで学習を進めていくことが可能です。

（1）授業環境

① 授業時には、教員が指導にあたりますが、コンピュータの技術的サポートは学内の技術員が担当するものとする。

② CALL設定されているコンピュータの操作は、学生証によってログオンするか、各自に与えられたパスワードの入力によるか、いずれかの手続きでログオンすれば、教材を直ちにサーバーから取り込むことができる。

③ 授業形態は1コマ90分とし、決められたシラバスに準じて学習を進められるが、進度は各自のペースで自由に学習する。また課題学習が毎回出される。

④ CALL教室の空き時間には、学習者が空き時間を利用して自主的に補習することができる態勢を整える。

（2）授業の進め方

① シラバスで学習教材の順序を周知させた上で、自由に学習を進めさせます。学習者側の責任で学習を進めていくため、習熟度により自由に学習を展開させることが可能で、学習者に満足感を与えることができます。

② 毎時間、シラバス通りに学習すべきレッスンを指定します。授業時間内にレッスンを終了できないとき、あるいは授業を欠席したときなどは、次週の授業時間までにレッスンを各自終了させておくことを義務づけます。シラバス通りに学習を進めていくため、学習者が同じ範囲を学習しますが、進度の速い人でもレッスンごとに十分な質問問題が用意されているため、時間を無駄にすることはありません。詳しくは、Linc Englishのカリキュラムの概要に教材内容、レッスン構成、問題数と流れの説明があるので参照してください。またLinc EnglishのHP（http://www.lincenglish.com）にアクセスして、トライアルにログインすると体験できるので問題構成を把握できます。

（3）授業モデル

［モデル1］

① はじめの5分で、テキストでその日の授業でカバーする演習（テキストでは〈Part〉とよぶ）のポイントや重要な英語表現のまとめをひと通り確認する（教師による一斉指導）。

② 次の5分で、今確認した知識をLinc English（1講座コンテンツ）で試す。

③ 次の3分で、今の②の解答を確認。

④ 次の5分で、上の②のLinc Englishに出てきた単語や語句、または文法事項をテキストで再度確認する（教師による一斉指導）。

⑤ 次の5分で、テキストのドリル問題に取り組ませて定着させる（この⑤の間、教師は巡回個別指導を行う）。

このような23分×2サイクル（2講座）を1回の授業とします。

（3）授業モデル
［モデル2］
① はじめの15分でその日行うレッスンのクイズをする（自主学習課題ですでに演習してある）。
② 次の10分は、テキストまたはＰＣを利用して、その日の授業でカバーするレッスのポイントや重要な英語表現のまとめをひと通り確認する（教師による一斉指導）。
③ 次の5分で、今確認した知識をLinc English（1講座コンテンツ）で試す。
④ 次の5分で、上の③のLinc Englishに出てきた単語や語句、または文法事項をテキストで再度確認する（教師による一斉指導）。
⑤ 次の5分で、テキストのドリル問題に取り組ませて定着させる（この⑤の間、教師は巡回個別指導を行う）。

このような40分×2サイクル（2講座）を1回の授業とします。

（速読読解練習の例）
オンラインの速読問題は、10行程度の文章に3問×4段落という構造になっていますので、その全体を7分程度で読み終えるようにします（カウントダウン制御機能があります）。授業ではテキストを利用して、10行程度の文章に2問、1段落のみを2分程度で読み終えるよう速度練習させます。次の演習として、10行程の文章に1問×4段落という全体を4分程度で読み終えるようにします。このような演習を繰り返すことで速読の力がつきます。この速読演習のあとに、読解演習にはいると、効果が期待できます。

（4）学習の評価
クイズやテストなどの結果の評価とともに、学習評価過程を評価することも重要です。常に学習目標や授業展開にフィードバックしていなければなりません。Linc Englishでは自己評価シートが作成できます。また学習過程の成果もファイルできます。教員もクラスごとに学習者の学習過程を把握できるし、Linc Englishの学習管理システムを利用してシラバスの情報、課題スケジュールの変更などのアナウンスメントもできるので非常に便利です。

以上がLinc Englishのカリキュラム概要・構成と本書の効果的な活用法です。しっかりとした英語運用能力を身につけるために、Linc Englishオンライン演習と本書を併用した学習を読者の皆様に強くお勧めします。また、一読だけではなく、自分に必要なところを再度選んで何回か学習を繰り返してみてください。

各レッスンの Part 1 Image Listening については、下記アドレスにアクセスし、音声を聞いて問題に答えてください。
http://audio.lincenglish.com

オンライン英語学習用テキスト
Linc English　Bronze Ⅱ

目　次

はじめに ………………………………………………………………………………………… *i*

本書の構成と効果的な使用法 …………………………………………………………………… *iii*

lesson 1

Part 1	Image Listening／写真描写問題 …………………………………………… *1*
Part 2	Question and Response／質疑応答問題 …………………………………… *2*
Part 3	Short Conversation／会話問題 …………………………………………… *3*
Part 4	Short Talks／説明文問題 ………………………………………………… *5*
Part 5	Reading／読解演習 ………………………………………………………… *7*
Part 6	Error Recognition／誤文訂正問題 ………………………………………… *9*
Part 7	Incomplete Sentence／文法・語彙問題 …………………………………… *10*

lesson 2

Part 1	Image Listening／写真描写問題 …………………………………………… *11*
Part 2	Question and Response／質疑応答問題 …………………………………… *12*
Part 3	Short Conversation／会話問題 …………………………………………… *13*
Part 4	Short Talks／説明文問題 ………………………………………………… *15*
Part 5	Reading／読解演習 ………………………………………………………… *17*
Part 6	Error Recognition／誤文訂正問題 ………………………………………… *19*
Part 7	Incomplete Sentence／文法・語彙問題 …………………………………… *20*

lesson 3

Part 1	Image Listening／写真描写問題 …………………………………………… *21*
Part 2	Question and Response／質疑応答問題 …………………………………… *22*
Part 3	Short Conversation／会話問題 …………………………………………… *23*
Part 4	Short Talks／説明文問題 ………………………………………………… *25*
Part 5	Reading／読解演習 ………………………………………………………… *26*
Part 6	Error Recognition／誤文訂正問題 ………………………………………… *28*
Part 7	Incomplete Sentence／文法・語彙問題 …………………………………… *29*

lesson 4

Part 1	Image Listening／写真描写問題 …………………………………………… *30*
Part 2	Question and Response／質疑応答問題 …………………………………… *31*
Part 3	Short Conversation／会話問題 …………………………………………… *32*
Part 4	Short Talks／説明文問題 ………………………………………………… *34*
Part 5	Reading／読解演習 ………………………………………………………… *35*
Part 6	Error Recognition／誤文訂正問題 ………………………………………… *37*
Part 7	Incomplete Sentence／文法・語彙問題 …………………………………… *38*

lesson 5

Part 1	Image Listening ／写真描写問題	39
Part 2	Question and Response ／質疑応答問題	40
Part 3	Short Conversation ／会話問題	41
Part 4	Short Talks ／説明文問題	43
Part 5	Reading ／読解演習	44
Part 6	Error Recognition ／誤文訂正問題	46
Part 7	Incomplete Sentence ／文法・語彙問題	48

lesson 6

Part 1	Image Listening ／写真描写問題	49
Part 2	Question and Response ／質疑応答問題	50
Part 3	Short Conversation ／会話問題	51
Part 4	Short Talks ／説明文問題	53
Part 5	Reading ／読解演習	54
Part 6	Error Recognition ／誤文訂正問題	56
Part 7	Incomplete Sentence ／文法・語彙問題	58

lesson 7

Part 1	Image Listening ／写真描写問題	59
Part 2	Question and Response ／質疑応答問題	60
Part 3	Short Conversation ／会話問題	61
Part 4	Short Talks ／説明文問題	63
Part 5	Reading ／読解演習	64
Part 6	Error Recognition ／誤文訂正問題	67
Part 7	Incomplete Sentence ／文法・語彙問題	68

lesson 8

Part 1	Image Listening ／写真描写問題	69
Part 2	Question and Response ／質疑応答問題	70
Part 3	Short Conversation ／会話問題	71
Part 4	Short Talks ／説明文問題	73
Part 5	Reading ／読解演習	74
Part 6	Error Recognition ／誤文訂正問題	76
Part 7	Incomplete Sentence ／文法・語彙問題	77

lesson 9

Part 1	Image Listening ／写真描写問題	78
Part 2	Question and Response ／質疑応答問題	79
Part 3	Short Conversation ／会話問題	80
Part 4	Short Talks ／説明文問題	82
Part 5	Reading ／読解演習	83
Part 6	Error Recognition ／誤文訂正問題	86
Part 7	Incomplete Sentence ／文法・語彙問題	87

lesson 10

Part 1	Image Listening ／写真描写問題	88
Part 2	Question and Response ／質疑応答問題	89
Part 3	Short Conversation ／会話問題	90
Part 4	Short Talks ／説明文問題	92
Part 5	Reading ／読解演習	93
Part 6	Error Recognition ／誤文訂正問題	96
Part 7	Incomplete Sentence ／文法・語彙問題	98

lesson 11

Part 1	Image Listening ／写真描写問題	99
Part 2	Question and Response ／質疑応答問題	100
Part 3	Short Conversation ／会話問題	101
Part 4	Short Talks ／説明文問題	103
Part 5	Reading ／読解演習	104
Part 6	Error Recognition ／誤文訂正問題	107
Part 7	Incomplete Sentence ／文法・語彙問題	109

lesson 12

Part 1	Image Listening ／写真描写問題	110
Part 2	Question and Response ／質疑応答問題	111
Part 3	Short Conversation ／会話問題	112
Part 4	Short Talks ／説明文問題	114
Part 5	Reading ／読解演習	115
Part 6	Error Recognition ／誤文訂正問題	118
Part 7	Incomplete Sentence ／文法・語彙問題	119

解　答 ･･ 120

オンライン英語学習用テキスト
Linc English　Bronze Ⅱ

Lesson 1　(http://audio.lincenglish.com にアクセスして音声を聞いてください)

Part 1　Image Listening／写真描写問題

1. 左の写真を見て、人物の行動や物の位置などについて文を3つ作りなさい。
　_____
　_____
　_____

2. 写真の描写文として最も適切な文をA～Dの中から選びなさい。
　(A), (B), (C), (D)

1. 左の写真を見て、人物の行動や物の位置などについて文を3つ作りなさい。
　_____
　_____
　_____

2. 写真の描写文として最も適切な文をA～Dの中から選びなさい。
　(A), (B), (C), (D)

1. 左の写真を見て、人物の行動や物の位置などについて文を3つ作りなさい。
　_____
　_____
　_____

2. 写真の描写文として最も適切な文をA～Dの中から選びなさい。
　(A), (B), (C), (D)

1. 左の写真を見て、人物の行動や物の位置などについて文を3つ作りなさい。
　_____
　_____
　_____

2. 写真の描写文として最も適切な文をA～Dの中から選びなさい。
　(A), (B), (C), (D)

Part 2　Question and Response／質疑応答問題

重要な質問表現

What is for dinner?
　「好きなもの」をきかれているのではなく、「今夜食るもの」をきかれている。

What happened to your car?
　車の外見についてではなく、起こったことことについてきかれている。

Can she play the guitar?
　主語は「彼女」で、ギターが弾けるかどうかが質問されている。

Did he give her flowers?
　「彼」が「彼女」に花をあげたかどうかが質問されている。誰が誰にあげるのかを混乱しないようにする。

Do you want some French fries with your hamburger?
　french fries は「フレンチ・フライ」、日本でいう「フライドポテト」である。

On what day is Halloween?
　ハロウィーンは何日かという質問（10月31日）である。

How is your family?
　how is ～で現在の状況をきいている。この場合、家族の様子（うまくやっているかどうか）をきいている。

Whose turn is it?
　名詞 turn は「順番」という意味をもつ。

When did they get married?
　結婚した年月日をきかれている。

How long is the flight from Montana to California?
　「移動時間」を答える質問である。

確認ドリル

次の1～5の質問に対して最も適切な応答をそれぞれ（A）～（C）の中から選びなさい。

1. What color are her eyes?
   (A)　Her eyes are beautiful.
   (B)　It is green.
   (C)　They are green.

2. What kind of music does Jenny like?
   (A)　She loves rock and roll.
   (B)　Jenny is a musician.
   (C)　She listens to music.

3. Can I please have five dollars?
   (A)　No, you don't.
   (B)　I don't need five dollars.
   (C)　No, I don't have any money.

4. Are you afraid of spiders?
   (A)　Yes, spiders are insects.
   (B)　No, I like spiders.
   (C)　Yes, spiders are afraid of me.

5. How is your family?
   (A)　My family is very important.
   (B)　My family is very big.
   (C)　My family is very good, thank you.

Part 3　Short Conversation／会話問題

次の会話を読んで、質問に最も適当な答えを選びなさい。

質問文パターン

＊ Where 型パターン

1. **A**：Hi, could I please speak to Sally?
   B：Sally's not here right now. Can I take a message?
   A：Could you please tell her to meet me at the park?

    Q：Where did this conversation take place?
    　　　a. In the park.　　　c. In the mall.
    　　　b. On the phone.　　d. At church.

   解説：take a message「伝言をうける」。

＊ How 型パターン

2. **A**：Oh no! There is a big mean dog!
   B：It's OK. Just stay calm.
   A：It's coming our way! Run!

    Q：How are the people acting?
    　　　a. Both people are very scared.　　　　　　　　　　c. One person is scared and one person likes to run.
    　　　b. One person is scared and one person is calm.　　d. Both people like the dog.

   解説：mean「意地悪な」。Come one's way「（ある人の通ろうとしている道へ）来る」。スピーカーBは犬を怖がるAを落ち着かせようとしている。

＊ What 型パターン

3. **A**：Do you want to go to the grocery store with me?
   B：Sure, but first let's go to rent a movie.
   A：O.K. We can go to the grocery store after we rent a movie.

    Q：What will the people do last?
    　　　a. Go rent a movie.　　　c. Go to the clothing store.
    　　　b. Go to the movie theater.　　d. Go to the grocery store.

   解説：grocery「食料品」。

* Why 型パターン

4. **A**：Wasn't that a great game?

   B：It was amazing! Our team did a great job!

   A：I'm so happy. Let's go get some ice cream!

   Q：Why will the people go to get ice cream?
   - a. To celebrate winning the game.
   - b. Because the team will go.
   - c. To meet some friends.
   - d. Because ice cream is not expensive.

解説：自分達のチームが試合に勝ったのでアイスクリームを食べに行こうといっている様子。

Part 4　Short Talks ／説明文問題

次の説明文の質問に最も適当な答えを選びなさい。

湖への家族旅行

Last weekend, I went to the lake with my family. It was a wonderful trip! We rented a boat. Then we had a barbecue and ate hamburgers and hot dogs. We saw many kinds of birds and some bison. The best part of the trip was when we stopped to pick some cherries from trees. I picked 12 pounds of cherries, which was enough to make a pie! At the end of the day we drove home and there was a beautiful sunset. I got a little sunburn, and that was the only bad part of the trip. Even though we were very tired, we were happy. It is a good memory for me.

1. What was her favorite part of the trip?
   a. When she saw birds and bison.
   b. When she saw the sunset.
   c. When her family was on the water.
   d. When they picked cherries from trees.

2. What was the only bad part of the trip?
   a. She got sunburn.
   b. She was tired.
   c. Her family didn't pick enough cherries.
   d. The birds ate the cherries.

解説：設問1　旅行の一番良かったこととして、「さくらんぼ摘み」が挙げられている。

　　　設問2　設問1と逆に、悪い思い出としては、「少し日焼けをしたこと」が挙げられている。(B)「疲れた」とは述べられているが、同時に「幸せだった」とあるので悪いこととしてはとらえられていないことがわかる。

ハンバーガー

Hamburgers are one of the most popular foods in the United States. No one can agree on who invented the hamburger, but we know that people have been eating them for over 200 years. A hamburger is a beef on bread with other toppings. Everyone has their own ideas about what toppings to put on their hamburgers. Many people like to put ketchup, mustard, pickles and onions on their hamburgers. My mother likes to add cheese, mayonnaise, lettuce and tomato. If you put cheese on a hamburger, it is called a cheeseburger. You can buy hamburgers at restaurants or barbecue them at home. In the summertime, you can smell hamburgers cooking on the barbecue in almost every town in the United States!

1. Where can you buy hamburgers?
   a. In summer.
   b. At restaurants.
   c. At home.
   d. Over 200 years.

2. Who invented the hamburger?
   a. His mother.
   b. McDonald's restaurant.
   c. Americans.
   d. No one can agree on it.

解説：設問1　ハンバーガーはレストランでも、またバーベキューをしても作れるもの。

設問2　No one can agree on ～「誰も～に同意することはできない」と2行目にあるので、誰がハンバーガーを作ったのかは不明である。

Part 5 Reading／読解演習

次の段落文を読み、各設問に対して最も適切な答えを選びなさい（各段落速読問題は2分以内に終わらせなさい）。

スピードリーディング

Karen Richards was born in Charlotte, North Carolina, in 1958. As a child, she grew up in a very small apartment with her mother, older brother, and elderly grandmother. There was only one bathroom, so everyone had to share the small space. Every morning, she and her brother raced to the bathroom to see who would have the first shower. Most of the time her brother, Samuel, slept on the couch in the living room to win the race.

1. Where did Karen grow up?
   a. In a house.
   b. In 1968.
   c. In a big apartment.
   d. In a small apartment.

2. How many bathrooms were there?
   a. More than one.
   b. Only one.
   c. Less than one.
   d. Two.

After high school, Karen moved to the west coast. When she was in high school, she had a dream. She wanted to buy and live in her own house, not an apartment. She worked two jobs in Seattle, Washington. Ms. Richards worked in a hospital during the day, and worked as a waitress at a local restaurant during the nights and on the weekends. Each month, she saved her money. Karen liked to work at the restaurant on Friday nights because she made a lot of money from the customers' tips.

1. What was Karen's dream?
   a. To live with her family.
   b. To buy an apartment.
   c. To live in Seattle.
   d. To buy a house.

2. Where did Karen work on the weekends?
   a. At a restaurant
   b. At a hospital
   c. At a Seattle bank
   d. At a high school

Finally, in 1990, Ms. Richards had enough money to buy a house. The house was perfect and in a great area of Seattle. She walked to work. She loved her house and wanted to spend more time there. So, in 1996, she started her own online business. She quit her day job but continued to work at the restaurant. Three years later, Karen had enough money from her at-home business. She stopped working at the restaurant and worked at home.

1. When did Karen start her online business?
   a. In 1990.
   b. In 1992.
   c. In 1996.
   d. In 1998.

2. What did Karen quit in 1996?
      a. Her day job.   c. Her job at the restaurant.
      b. Her night job.   d. Her online business.

スピードリーディングと同じ文を読み、各設問に対して最も適切な答えを選びなさい。

読解問題

Karen Richards was born in Charlotte, North Carolina, in 1958. As a child, she grew up in a very small apartment with her mother, older brother, and elderly grandmother. There was only one bathroom, so everyone had to share the small space. Every morning, she and her brother raced to the bathroom to see who would have the first shower. Most of the time her brother, Samuel, slept on the couch in the living room to win the race.

After high school, Karen moved to the west coast. When she was in high school, she had a dream. She wanted to buy and live in her own house, not an apartment. She worked two jobs in Seattle, Washington. Ms. Richards worked in a hospital during the day, and worked as a waitress at a local restaurant during the nights and on the weekends. Each month, she saved her money. Karen liked to work at the restaurant on Friday nights because she made a lot of money from the customers' tips.

Finally, in 1990, Ms. Richards had enough money to buy a house. The house was perfect and in a great area of Seattle. She walked to work. She loved her house and wanted to spend more time there. So, in 1996, she started her own online business. She quit her day job but continued to work at the restaurant. Three years later, Karen had enough money from her at-home business. She stopped working at the restaurant and worked at home.

Karen's dream came true. However, it took a lot of time, patience, and hard work. She learned how to type quickly and how to use new computer programs. She works hard, but Ms. Richards now finds time to enjoy her new life. Last year, she repainted her house and planted flowers in her back yard. Her next house project will be to re-do her bathroom so there is more space.

Comprehension Questions

1. Why did Karen and her brother race to the bathroom?
      a. To go to the bathroom.   c. To get the first shower.
      b. To wash their face.   d. To wash their hands.

2. Why did Karen save money each month?
      a. To buy a car.   c. To buy an apartment.
      b. To buy a house.   d. To buy a dog.

3. What year did Karen have enough money from her at-home business?
      a. 1992.   c. 1997.
      b. 1995.   d. 1999.

4. In paragraph 4, the last sentence, the word 're-do' means:
      a. To paint.   c. To make smaller.
      b. To do again.   d. To sell the house.

Part 6 Error Recognition／誤文訂正問題

各文には文法的誤りがあります。訂正もしくは書き換えを必要とする語や語句を選びなさい。

1. Craig is the smartest students in the entire class.
    　　　　　A　　　B　　　　C　　　　D

    解説：主語 Craig は単数である。よって、下線 C の students に複数形 -s は不必要となる。

    正しい英文：Craig is the smartest student in the entire class.

2. The strange man was talking to both my friend and I.
    　　　　A　　　　　　B　　　　C　　　　　　　D

    解説：下線 D の語 I には前置詞 to が掛かっている。よって、前置詞を受ける人称（代）名詞は目的格の形をとる。よって、下線 D には I の目的格 me が置かれる。

    正しい英文：The strange man was talking to both my friend and me.

3. Unless you have fifteen dollars, you will buy the book.
    　　A　　　　　B　　　　　　　　　　　C　　　D

    解説：意味内容的に cannot が下線 C に置かれる。訳参照。（注釈：unless（接続詞）：〜でなければ）

    正しい英文：Unless you have fifteen dollars, you cannot buy the book.

4. That diamond necklace belongs to me. It is my.
    　　　　A　　　　　　　　　　　B　　C　　D

    解説：1文目の意味内容から、下線 D には I の所有代名詞 mine（私のもの）が適切である。また、所有格 my は名詞の前に置かれなければならない。例：my watch：私の時計

    正しい英文：That diamond necklace belongs to me. It is mine.

5. Maki always going shopping on the weekends.
    　　　　　A　　　　B　　　C　　　D

    解説：キーワード、always と on the weekends に注目しよう。「習慣的事柄」がここでは述べられているので、動詞は現在形であることが適切である。よって、下線 A は現在形の動詞 goes が適切となる。

    正しい英文：Maki always goes shopping on the weekends.

6. I was listening to music when the mailman was coming.
    　　　　A　　　B　　　　　　　C　　　　　　　D

    解説：意味内容から、下線 D は動詞の過去形が適切である。訳参照。過去進行形（was coming）では意味が通らない。

    正しい英文：I was listening to music when the mailman came.

7. Angela is so thoughtful. She always writes to mine.
    　　　　A　　B　　　　　　　　　　　C　　　　D

    解説：所有代名詞 mine（私のもの）の代わりとなる名詞が文中にないため不可となる。

    正しい英文：Angela is so thoughtful. She always writes to me.

Part 7　Incomplete Sentence／文法・語彙問題

文法的に適切な語句を1つ選び、文を完成させなさい。

1. I have been in Seattle _____ 2001.
    a. for　　　c. since
    b. because　d. until

    訳：私は2001年からシアトルに住んでいる。
    解説：since：〜以来　sinceと現在完了（have（has）＋過去分詞）は呼応して使われるときが多いので注意しよう。

2. When the phone rang, Susan _____ television.
    a. watching　　c. watched
    b. watches　　d. was watching

    訳：その電話が鳴ったとき、スーザンはテレビを見ていた。
    解説：副詞説（when the phone…）と主節（Susan…）の事柄が同時に起こっていたと推測できるので、過去進行形 d. was watching が空欄に入る最も適切な語となる。訳参照。

3. Is this your first time in Rome, or have you been here _____?
    a. yet　　c. next
    b. then　d. before

    訳：ローマは今回が初めてですか？　それとも、以前ここへ来たことがありますか？
    解説：意味内容から、「経験」を表す関係代名詞が使われていると推測できるので、副詞 d. before（以前）が空欄に入る。

4. John likes _____ a shower in the evening.
    a. take　　c. make
    b. to take　d. to make

    訳：ジョンは夜にシャワーを浴びるのが好きだ。
    解説：like to do (-ing)：〜するのが好きだ　take a shower：シャワーを浴びる。

5. Brian _____ play the piano everyday.
    a. didn't don't used to　　c. use to
    b. did use to　　　　　　d. used to

    訳：ブライアンはかつて毎日ピアノを弾いていた。
    解説：used to do：かつてはよく〜したものだ　did not use to do：かつては〜しなかった。

Lesson 2 (http://audio.lincenglish.com にアクセスして音声を聞いてください)

Part 1　Image Listening／写真描写問題

1. 左の写真を見て、人物の行動や物の位置などについて文を3つ作りなさい。
   _____
   _____
   _____

2. 写真の描写文として最も適切な文をA～Dの中から選びなさい。
   (A), (B), (C), (D)

1. 左の写真を見て、人物の行動や物の位置などについて文を3つ作りなさい。
   _____
   _____
   _____

2. 写真の描写文として最も適切な文をA～Dの中から選びなさい。
   (A), (B), (C), (D)

1. 左の写真を見て、人物の行動や物の位置などについて文を3つ作りなさい。
   _____
   _____
   _____

2. 写真の描写文として最も適切な文をA～Dの中から選びなさい。
   (A), (B), (C), (D)

1. 左の写真を見て、人物の行動や物の位置などについて文を3つ作りなさい。
   _____
   _____
   _____

2. 写真の描写文として最も適切な文をA～Dの中から選びなさい。
   (A), (B), (C), (D)

Part 2　Question and Response／質疑応答問題

重要な質問表現

What did you name your new baby?
　　name は動詞で「～と名づける」という意味もある。

What did you think of that movie?
　　映画の感想をきかれている。

Why haven't you told me your secret?
　　why「なぜ」と言われていることから、適切な答えとなるのは秘密を言わなかった理由、またはこれから秘密を言うつもりがあるかないかの意思表示である。

Has he ever played American football?
　　has he ever played は過去完了形で、答えもこの形を持続する。

Would you like to meet my new friend?
　　would you like to ～「～したいですか」の返答は I would like to ～「～したいです」となる。

Who called you on the phone?
　　電話をあなたに「かけてきた」人は誰かときかれている。

Do you mind if I sit here?
　　do you mind ～「～することを気にしますか」に対する答えは yes の場合「はい、気にします（～をしないでください）」、または no「いいえ、気にしません（どうぞそうしてください）」となる。

Do you have any time to go to the coffee shop with me?
　　ここでは時間がきかれているのではなく、「一緒に喫茶店に行く時間があるかどうか」がきかれている。

That woman has nine children, right?
　　「あの女性」に子どもが9人いるかどうかについて確認している。

Could you please tell me where I can find the library?
　　"could you please tell me where I can find ～?" は道を尋ねる1つの表現である。

確認ドリル

次の1～5の質問に対して最も適切な応答をそれぞれ（A）～（C）の中から選びなさい。

1. How has she been?
   (A)　She has gone to the mall.
   (B)　She has been sick.
   (C)　She is playing volleyball.

2. Have you ever been to the United States?
   (A)　No, I've never been there.
   (B)　Yes, I want to go.
   (C)　No, I went there two years ago.

3. How long have you been here?
   (A)　I have been here for 20 minutes.
   (B)　I have been here three times before.
   (C)　I am late.

4. Would you like to go out to a restaurant for dinner?
   (A)　Dinner is at the restaurant.
   (B)　I've never seen it before.
   (C)　I can't tonight. My father wants me to come home now.

5. You look familiar. ave we met before?
   (A)　I think we met at the office.
   (B)　She likes to meet people.
   (C)　I haven't met her before.

Part 3　Short Conversation／会話問題

次の会話を読んで、質問に最も適当な答えを選びなさい。

質問文パターン

* What 型パターン

1. **A**：Are you going to cook?
   B：Yes, but first we must buy some eggs.
   A：Oh, actually I already bought some.

   Q：What do they need to buy in order to cook?
   　　a. They must buy some eggs.　　　c. They need to buy many groceries.
   　　b. They don't need to buy anything.　　d. They don't know what they need to buy.

   解説：料理に必要なものは「卵」である。

* Where 型パターン

2. **A**：Ouch! An insect just stung me!
   B：A mosquito bit me, too.
   A：Let's move our picnic away from the river.

   Q：Where are the people having a picnic?
   　　a. They are having a picnic too　　c. They are having a picnic too far away
   　　　close to the river.　　　　　　　　from the river.
   　　b. They are having a picnic inside.　d. They are having a picnic where there is no river.

   解説：stung は sting「（虫が）刺す」の過去形である。川の近くに場所をとったので蚊がたくさんきて、困っているようだ。

* How 型パターン

3. **A**：You won't believe what happened to me yesterday!
   B：I know. You fell into the river!
   A：Oh, Ryan must have told you.

   Q：How does the person know about what happened?
   　　a. Ryan told him.　　　　c. He doesn't believe Ryan.
   　　b. He heard it on the news.　d. He saw it happen.

   解説：Ryan must have told you の must は「〜に違いない」という当然の推定を表している。

* Why 型パターン

4. **A**：Are you interested in politics?
   B：Yes, I like to know what is going on in the government.
   A：So do I.

   Q：Why do they like politics?
       a. Because they like to listen to the government.
       b. Because they like to know what is happening in the government.
       c. Because they like politicians.
       d. Because they like to watch politics on television.

解説：政府内で何が起きているかに興味があるからと理由づけされている。

Part 4 Short Talks／説明文問題

次の説明文の質問に最も適当な答えを選びなさい。

アリとキリギリス

Have you ever heard the story of the ant and the grasshopper? The grasshopper liked to have fun all of the time. The ant knew that it was important to be responsible. In the summer, the ant spent time saving food in his house so that he would have enough to eat during the cold winter months. The grasshopper played every day and didn't save any food for himself. When winter came, the ant had enough food to last until spring. The grasshopper didn't have enough food, and sadly, he didn't live through the winter. The lesson in this story is that although it is fun to play, it is important to be responsible, too.

1. How are the ant and the grasshopper different in the story?
    a. The ant was not responsible, whereas the grasshopper was responsible.
    b. The grasshopper only wanted to have fun, whereas the ant was responsible.
    c. They were both responsible.
    d. They both only wanted to have fun.

2. What happened to the grasshopper?
    a. He moved away.
    b. He played all winter long.
    c. He died.
    d. He moved in with the ant.

解説：設問1　キリギリスは毎日楽しく過ごしているだけであるが、一方のアリは毎日自分の食べ物のために働く働きもので責任感もある。
設問2　キリギリスは食べ物を蓄えることをしなかったので、生き延びることができなかった。Live through winter「冬を（通し）過ごす」。

アメリカ人のペット好き

Americans love to have pets. In the United States, more than half of all households have a family pet. There are more than 180 million domestic animals in the world. Dogs and cats are the most popular pets, followed by horses and birds. Some people even have reptiles like snakes, lizards and turtles! Cats can be indoor cats or outdoor cats. Americans like to take their dogs for walks outside, camping and on drives. In some cultures, dogs are only for security or working, but in the U.S. dogs are part of the family. A famous saying is, "A dog is a man's best friend."

1. How do Americans feel about their pets?
    a. They are part of the family.
    b. They are for security and working only.
    c. They are not important.
    d. There are too many pets.

2. Which of the following is a reptile?
    a. A cat.
    b. A dog.
    c. A horse.
    d. A lizard.

解説：設問1　アメリカ人のペットに対する感情は人間に対してと同じものである。つまりは人間同様として扱っている。

設問2　爬虫類は、文中でも説明があるが「ヘビ・トカゲ・カメ」などである。

Part 5 Reading／読解演習

次の段落文を読み、各設問に対して最も適切な答えを選びなさい（各段落速読問題は2分以内に終わらせなさい）。

スピードリーディング

Over the past thirty years, the workplace has changed. The majority of women used to stay home, while the men went to work. Today, the workplace is not for men only. In fact, 76 percent of women work outside of the home. There are more than two million stay-at-home dads. Many women wear the business suits and provide income for the family.

1. What has changed over the past thirty years?
   a. Women.
   b. Children.
   c. The school.
   d. The workplace.

2. How many dads stay at home?
   a. Over two million.
   b. Over two hundred.
   c. Less than two thousand.
   d. Exactly twenty thousand.

Mark Thompson is a writer, a husband, and a father. Mark's nickname is Mr. Mom because he is a stay-at-home dad. When he has time, which is usually before his two kids wake up, he works on his book that he is writing. He is writing about the changes and responsibilities in the home. His wife's name is Marion. She is a lawyer and makes a lot of money. Mark does not have a high paying job, so he takes care of the children, David and Lilly.

1. What is Mark's nickname?
   a. Marcus.
   b. Mr. Thompson.
   c. Mr. Mom.
   d. Stay-at-home.

2. What are the names of the Thompson's children?
   a. Marion and Mark.
   b. David and Marion.
   c. David and Lilly.
   d. Marion and Lilly.

Mark stays extremely busy. He has work responsibilities. He also has house responsibilities. He needs to keep the house clean, do the cooking, and take the children to school. Fortunately, the children take the bus home from school, giving Mark more time at home. Marion has responsibilities at work and at home also. She has to arrive at work by 7:30 a.m. She has important meetings, and she has to type reports to her boss. Although she is not home a lot during the week, she spends her weekend with her family.

1. When does Marion get to work?
   a. At 8:00 a.m.
   b. At 7:30 a.m.
   c. After she takes the kids to school.
   d. After breakfast.

2. What does Marion do on the weekends?
    a. She works at the office.
    b. She has responsibilities at work.
    c. She spends time with her family.
    d. She cleans the house with Mark.

スピードリーディングと同じ文を読み、各設問に対して最も適切な答えを選びなさい。

読解問題

Over the past thirty years, the workplace has changed. The majority of women used to stay home, while the men went to work. Today, the workplace is not for men only. In fact, 76 percent of women work outside of the home. There are more than two million stay-at-home dads. Many women wear the business suits and provide income for the family.

Mark Thompson is a writer, a husband, and a father. Mark's nickname is Mr. Mom because he is a stay-at-home dad. When he has time, which is usually before his two kids wake up, he works on his book that he is writing. He is writing about the changes and responsibilities in the home. His wife's name is Marion. She is a lawyer and makes a lot of money. Mark does not have a high paying job, so he takes care of the children, David and Lilly.

Mark stays extremely busy. He has work responsibilities. He also has house responsibilities. He needs to keep the house clean, do the cooking, and take the children to school. Fortunately, the children take the bus home from school, giving Mark more time at home. Marion has responsibilities at work and at home also. She has to arrive at work by 7:30 a.m. She has important meetings, and she has to type reports to her boss. Although she is not home a lot during the week, she spends her weekend with her family.

Mark and Marion are happily married. They have been married for eight years. They used to live in the country, but because of Marion's job, they moved to the city. They have difficult jobs and sometimes there are problems. They both have a lot of responsibilities and very little time to relax. However, the family communicates well, and the children understand.

Comprehension Questions

1. What do more than half of women do today?
    a. Stay at home.
    b. Clean the house.
    c. Go to work.
    d. Raise the children.

2. What is Mark's occupation?
    a. A writer.
    b. A lawyer.
    c. A teacher.
    d. Mr. Mom.

3. What does Marion have to do for her boss?
    a. Go to meetings.
    b. Type reports.
    c. Clean the house.
    d. Get coffee.

4. What do Mark and Marion have little time for?
    a. To relax.
    b. To communicate.
    c. To move.
    d. To be happily married.

Part 6　Error Recognition／誤文訂正問題

各文には文法的誤りがあります。訂正もしくは書き換えを必要とする語句を選びなさい。

1. Peggy is <u>on</u> the mood <u>for</u> a good movie. She <u>loves</u> comedies.
   　　　　　　A　　　　　　　B　　　　　　C　　　　　D

   解説：be in the mood for ～：～な気分だ
   正しい英文：Peggy is in the mood for a good movie. She loves comedies.

2. <u>At</u> 4:30, Miranda <u>remembered</u> <u>to</u> call <u>her's</u> doctor.
   　A　　　　　　　　　B　　　　　　C　　　　　D

   解説：主格 she の正しい所有格の形は her（彼女の）である。
   正しい英文：At 4:30, Miranda remembered to call her doctor.

3. The <u>French</u> teachers should <u>really</u> <u>talk</u> more <u>slow</u>.
   　　　　A　　　　　　　　　　B　　　　C　　　　　D

   解説：ここでは、意味内容的に副詞 slowly（ゆっくり）が適切である。
   正しい英文：The French teachers should really talk more slowly.

4. I need to <u>take</u> a shower. <u>My</u> hair <u>is</u> <u>dirt</u>.
   　　　　　　A　　　　　　　　B　　　　　C　D

   解説：意味内容に注意。ここでは、名詞 dirt（汚れ）ではなく、形容詞 dirty（汚い）が適切である。
   正しい英文：I need to take a shower. My hair is dirty.

5. After work, my aunt <u>needs</u> to fill <u>in</u> <u>her</u> car <u>with</u> unleaded gasoline.
   　　　　　　　　　　　A　　　　　　　B　C　　　　D

   解説：fill up with：（車を）（ガソリン）で満タンにする。
   正しい英文：After work, my aunt needs to fill up her car with unleaded gasoline.

6. During <u>yesterday's</u> class the professor <u>gave</u> <u>us</u> a lot of <u>informations</u> about grammar.
   　　　　　　A　　　　　　　　　　　　　B　　C　　　　　　　D

   解説：information（情報）は不可算名詞。よって、複数形 -s は不要となる。
   正しい英文：During yesterday's class the professor gave us a lot of information about grammar.

7. My uncle <u>isn't</u> crazy <u>to</u> seafood. However, my aunt <u>loves</u> <u>it</u>.
   　　　　　　A　　　　　　B　　　　　　　　　　　　　　C　　D

   解説：crazy about（for/over/on）～：～に夢中だ
   正しい英文：My uncle isn't crazy about seafood. However, my aunt loves it.

Part 7 Incomplete Sentence／文法・語彙問題

文法的に適切な語句を1つ選び、文を完成させなさい。

1. Tom _____ in New York for two years, but now he lives in Boston.
   - a. lived
   - b. has lived
   - c. did lived
   - d. had been living

   訳：トムは2年間ニューヨークに住んだが、今はボストンに住んでいる。
   解説：意味内容に注意。過去と現在の出来事の対比が表されている。訳参照。

2. Nicole _____ to the party.
   - a. invites
   - b. has invited
   - c. is invited
   - d. invited

   訳：ニコールはそのパーティーに招待されている。
   解説：意味内容的に受動態（be動詞＋過去分詞）が使われなければならない。よって、c. is invited が空欄に入る最も適切な語。受動態は日本語で「Sが〜される」と考える。

3. Have you _____ your homework yet?
   - a. finish
   - b. finished
   - c. been finished
   - d. finishes

   訳：もう宿題を済ましましたか？
   解説：ここでは現在完了形（have（has）＋過去完了）が使われているため、空欄には必然的に動詞の過去完了 b. finished が入る。

4. I don't like to watch movies, so I hardly _____ go to the theater.
   - a. never
   - b. ever
   - c. don't
   - d. not

   訳：私は映画鑑賞が好きではない。だからほとんど映画館に行かない。
   解説：hardly ever：ほとんど〜ない

5. When I was young, I _____ like fruit.
   - a. didn't using to
   - b. did use to
   - c. use to
   - d. didn't used to

   訳：私は若かった頃、果物が好きではなかった。
   解説：did not used to do：かつて〜でなかった

Lesson 3 (http://audio.lincenglish.com にアクセスして音声を聞いてください)

Part 1　Image Listening／写真描写問題

1. 左の写真を見て、人物の行動や物の位置などについて文を3つ作りなさい。
   _____
   _____
   _____

2. 写真の描写文として最も適切な文をA～Dの中から選びなさい。
   (A), (B), (C), (D)

1. 左の写真を見て、人物の行動や物の位置などについて文を3つ作りなさい。
   _____
   _____
   _____

2. 写真の描写文として最も適切な文をA～Dの中から選びなさい。
   (A), (B), (C), (D)

1. 左の写真を見て、人物の行動や物の位置などについて文を3つ作りなさい。
   _____
   _____
   _____

2. 写真の描写文として最も適切な文をA～Dの中から選びなさい。
   (A), (B), (C), (D)

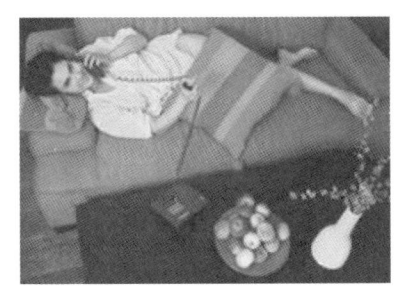

1. 左の写真を見て、人物の行動や物の位置などについて文を3つ作りなさい。
   _____
   _____
   _____

2. 写真の描写文として最も適切な文をA～Dの中から選びなさい。
   (A), (B), (C), (D)

Part 2　Question and Response／質疑応答問題

重要な質問表現

Has Shane eaten Mexican food more than once?
　　「食べたことがある」かどうか過去完了の経験が問われている。

Did you get the pictures I sent to you?
　　get「得る」の同義語は receive「受け取る」。

How do you like the food?
　　How do you like ～は何かに対しての感想・意見をきくときの表現である。

I don't have any bread. Could you please buy some for me at the store?
　　パンを買ってきて欲しいというリクエストに対応する。

I heard they had an accident. Are they okay?
　　事故にあった「彼ら」の様子を心配している。

What will Jason do tomorrow?
　　「明日」の予定をきいているので、時制は未来形にする。

Have you ever gone camping outside before?
　　キャンプをしたことがあるかどうかの「経験」を問われている。

Did you put the food in the refrigerator?
　　refrigerator「冷蔵庫」に食べ物をいれたかどうかの確認である。

Is your brother on a football team?
　　動詞は is なので、応答も is を含んだものです。be on a team「チームに入る」。

Do you know that you broke my heart?
　　break one's heart は「（言い争いなどで）心を傷つける」という意味で失恋の場合などの内面的・精神的損傷に使われる。

確認ドリル

次の 1～5 の質問に対して最も適切な応答をそれぞれ（A）～（C）の中から選びなさい。

1. I really love to eat sweets. How about you?
   (A) I think so.
   (B) Me neither.
   (C) Me too.

2. Why didn't you invite Amy to the party?
   (A) Amy doesn't like parties.
   (B) I can invite many friends.
   (C) Amy invited her friends.

3. Would you rather see a funny movie or a romantic movie?
   (A) My friend saw a scary movie.
   (B) Movies are fun.
   (C) I would prefer a funny movie.

4. How old were you when you started to talk?
   (A) I am a baby.
   (B) I am 15 years old.
   (C) I was only one year old.

5. Would you like some ice cream?
   (A) No, I don't care.
   (B) I didn't eat it.
   (C) No, thanks. I'm not hungry.

Part 3　Short Conversation／会話問題

次の会話を読んで、質問に最も適当な答えを選びなさい。

質問文パターン

＊Who 型パターン

1. **A**：You haven't paid your rent yet.
   B：I'm sorry. I have a lot of bills to pay this month.
   A：Well, you are a good tenant so you can pay the rent next week.

   Q：Who is having this conversation?
   　　　a. A child and an adult.　　　c. Two co-workers.
   　　　b. A tenant and a landlord.　　d. A mother and her son.

   解説：家賃について大家さんと話している様子。

＊Why 型パターン

2. **A**：My tooth has hurt for three days.
   B：Have you gone to the dentist?
   A：No, I am afraid of dentists, but maybe I will go tomorrow.

   Q：Why doesn't she want to go to the dentist?
   　　　a. Because she likes dentists.　　　　　　　　c. Because she is afraid of the dentist.
   　　　b. Because she thinks dentists are not nice.　d. Because her tooth hurts.

   解説：I am afraid of dentists「歯医者が怖い」と言っている。

＊What 型パターン

3. **A**：Please tell her that Joyce Johnson called. I will call her again tomorrow.
   B：I will leave the message for her.
   A：Thank you so much.

   Q：What is happening?
   　　　a. Joyce is leaving a message for someone else.　c. Joyce cannot take the call.
   　　　b. Joyce just received a phone call.　　　　　　d. Joyce's friend is calling her.

   解説：電話にでたスピーカー B が伝言を預かっている。

＊Where 型パターン

4. **A**：Please fill it up with gasoline.
   B：Would you like me to wash your windshield too?
   A：No, thank you. I can do it myself.

Q：Where are the people?
- a. At the park.
- b. At the grocery store.
- c. At the car wash.
- d. At the gas station.

解説：「ガソリン」「正面ガラス」「洗う」から連想できるのは（D）である。アメリカでは、（C）洗車場とガソリンをいれる場所は別になっている。

Part 4　Short Talks／説明文問題

次の説明文の質問に最も適当な答えを選びなさい。

節約

My mom likes to go shopping on Saturdays, because that is the day that everything is on sale. Every Saturday we go to the supermarket. My mom brings a list of the things we need to buy. She also brings coupons to save even more money. She always pays with cash, because she doesn't like to use credit cards. Last week we got five pounds of hamburger for only five dollars! Mom says that it is good to save your money, so if you shop carefully, you can have money for other things. I told her that we should buy a swimming pool with all the money she saved. She didn't like that idea.

1. What does her mom bring to the supermarket on Saturdays?
   - a. Her dog.
   - b. Her coupons and a list.
   - c. Her credit card.
   - d. Her mother.

2. What does her mom like to do with money?
   - a. Spend it.
   - b. Give it away.
   - c. Buy a swimming pool.
   - d. Save it.

解説：設問1　母は買い物に a list of things「買い物リスト」と節約のための coupons「割引券」を持って行くとある。

設問2　お金を節約する、つまりは save「貯める」ことが好きなのだ。

スコッティと父親

When Scotty was a child, his father used to take him to baseball games every month. They would buy popcorn, peanuts and hot dogs, and drink big sodas. Their favorite team was the Seattle Seahawks. Scotty always looked forward to this special time with his father. Now, Scotty is an adult and he has a son of his own. Continuing the family tradition, Scotty now takes his son to the baseball games. They eat all the same food as Scotty and his father used to eat.

1. What do Scotty and his son eat at the games?
   - a. Ice cream.
   - b. Peanuts, hot dogs and popcorn.
   - c. Hamburgers.
   - d. Cheese.

2. Why does Scotty take his son to the baseball games?
   - a. Because his son doesn't like baseball.
   - b. Because he wants to eat hotdogs.
   - c. Because he wants to continue the family tradition.
   - d. Because he doesn't want to stay at home.

解説：設問1　スコッティが彼の父親とかつて食べていたものを野球観戦時に自分の子どもとも食べている。それらは「ポップコーン・ピーナッツ・ホットドッグ」である。

設問2　スコッティの父親がそうしていたように、スコッティ自身も同じことを息子にして、家族の伝統を受け継いでいる。

Part 5 Reading／読解演習

次の段落文を読み、各設問に対して最も適切な答えを選びなさい（各段落速読問題は 2 分以内に終わらせなさい）。

スピードリーディング

In the United States, many children go to preschool at age three. Most children begin elementary school at age five. They enter high school as a freshman at age fourteen, and they graduate high school four years later. Most college students earn a degree at age twenty-one.

1. Where do children usually go at age three in the United States?
   a. Elementary school.   c. To daycare.
   b. Preschool.   d. To their grandma's house.

2. What age do Americans enter high school?
   a. At age eighteen.   c. As a freshman.
   b. At age twelve.   d. At age fourteen.

Douglas Bishop is not an average child. He is extremely smart. He began reading when he was eight months old. By the time he was three years old, he was reading fifth-grade books and learning algebra. He started high school when he was five. However, he was too smart for high school and often felt bored in class. His mind was ahead of the other students.

1. What is a person who is extremely smart called?
   a. Average.   c. A child.
   b. A genius.   d. Algebra.

2. When did Douglas begin learning algebra?
   a. When he was in fifth grade.   c. When he finished high school.
   b. When he was three.   d. When he was five.

When he was six, he studied at a small college in Ohio. Two years later he transferred to a bigger university. He earned a bachelor's degree in biochemistry and mathematics at age ten. He continued with his education. He received his master's degree in geology, the study of the earth and the environment.

1. What happened to Doug at age ten?
   a. He went to high school.   c. He got his bachelor's degree.
   b. He went to a bigger university.   d. He transferred from Ohio.

2. In what subject did he receive a master's degree?
   a. Mathematics.   c. Education.
   b. Geology.   d. Biochemistry.

スピードリーディングと同じ文を読み、各設問に対して最も適切な答えを選びなさい。

読解問題

In the United States, many children go to preschool at age three. Most children begin elementary school at age five. They enter high school as a freshman at age fourteen, and they graduate high school four years later. Most college students earn a degree at age twenty-one.

Douglas Bishop is not an average child. He is extremely smart. He began reading when he was eight months old. By the time he was three years old, he was reading fifth-grade books and learning algebra. He started high school when he was five. However, he was too smart for high school and often felt bored in class. His mind was ahead of the other students.

When he was six, he studied at a small college in Ohio. Two years later he transferred to a bigger university. He earned a bachelor's degree in biochemistry and mathematics at age ten. He continued with his education. He received his master's degree in geology, the study of the earth and the environment.

Douglas is still studying. He loves to learn and to apply his knowledge to the real world. In his free time, he enjoys reading books more than watching action movies. Right now, he is only fourteen years old, but he has career plans. In the near future, he wants to work for Microsoft and perhaps also become a college professor. His knowledge can take him many places.

Comprehension Questions

1. What do children begin at age five in the U.S.?
    a. A degree.
    b. Elementary school.
    c. Junior high school.
    d. Mathematics.

2. How did Douglas feel in class?
    a. Bored.
    b. Smart.
    c. Ahead.
    d. Happy.

3. In the second sentence in paragraph three, the word "transferred" has the closest meaning to:
    a. Lived.
    b. Moved.
    c. Walked.
    d. Studied.

4. What does Douglas want to be when he is older?
    a. A writer.
    b. A geologist.
    c. A professor.
    d. A doctor.

Part 6　Error Recognition／誤文訂正問題

各文には文法的誤りがあります。訂正もしくは書き換えを必要とする語句を選びなさい。

1. Yesterday I <u>missed</u> the bus <u>to</u> school because I <u>leaved</u> the house <u>at</u> 7:30.
　　　　　　　　A　　　　　　　　B　　　　　　　　　　　C　　　　　　　　D

　　解説：動詞 leave（〜を去る）の過去形は left。

　　正しい英文：Yesterday I missed the bus to school because I left the house at 7:30.

2. <u>What</u> big cities <u>have</u> Nancy <u>visited</u> <u>in</u> Italy last summer?
　　　A　　　　　　　B　　　　　　C　　 D

　　解説：この文での主語は Nancy（固有名詞）のため、その主語の助動詞は has になっていなければならない。

　　正しい英文：What big cities has Nancy visited in Italy last summer?

3. My parents wanted <u>I</u> <u>to study</u> engineering, but I'm <u>studying</u> business <u>at</u> Yale.
　　　　　　　　　　　A　　　B　　　　　　　　　　　　　　　　C　　　　　　　　D

　　解説：動詞の直後に続く語は目的語である。よって、動詞 wanted の後に続く一人称の名詞は目的格 me となる。

　　正しい英文：My parents wanted me to study engineering, but I'm studying business at Yale

4. This homework is <u>much</u> <u>difficult</u>. Can you please help <u>me</u> with <u>it</u>?
　　　　　　　　　　　A　　　　B　　　　　　　　　　　　　　　　C　　　　　　D

　　解説：副詞 much は形容詞を直接修飾できない。よって、ここでは形容詞 difficult を修飾できる副詞が適切である。

　　正しい英文：This homework is too difficult. Can you please help me with it?

5. You are going <u>to miss</u> the <u>important</u> meeting! You need <u>to</u> hurry <u>on</u>!
　　　　　　　　　　A　　　　　　　B　　　　　　　　　　　　　　　　C　　　　　D

　　解説：hurry up：急ぐ（通例、命令文とともに使われることが多い）

　　正しい英文：You are going to miss the important meeting! You need to hurry up!

6. I never used <u>work</u> <u>late</u>, but now I have <u>many</u> assignments from <u>my</u> boss.
　　　　　　　　　A　　　B　　　　　　　　　　　　C　　　　　　　　　　　　　D

　　解説：used to do：かつて〜していた（過去の規則的習慣）

　　正しい英文：I never used to work late, but now I have many assignments from my boss.

7. <u>Put</u> the applications <u>on</u> Mike's desk. <u>They</u> needs to read <u>them</u> by 3:00.
　　A　　　　　　　　　　　B　　　　　　　　　　　C　　　　　　　　　　D

　　解説：主語 they の後に続く現在形の動詞には三人称単数現在形 -s は不必要。

　　正しい英文：Put the applications on Mike's desk. He needs to read them by 3:00.

Part 7　Incomplete Sentence／文法・語彙問題

文法的に適切な語句を1つ選び、文を完成させなさい。

1. Did you clean the house all by _____.
   - a. herself
   - b. hers
   - c. yours
   - d. yourself

訳：たった1人で部屋の掃除をしたの？
解説：all by oneself：たった1人で文の主語がyouであることからその再帰代名詞は必然的にyourselfとなる。よって、d. yourselfが空欄に入る最も適切な語。

2. _____ I missed the bus, I was late for class.
   - a. Even
   - b. So
   - c. If
   - d. Since

訳：バスを逃したので、授業に遅れた。
解説：意味内容に注意。ここで使われるd. Since（〜なので）は「理由」を導く接続詞となる。

3. Of all the books I've read, The Notebook is _____.
   - a. the romantic
   - b. the most romantic
   - c. best book romance
   - d. better

訳：これまで読んだすべての本の中で、「ザ・ノートブック」が最もロマンチックだ。
解説：文脈から空欄には最上級が入る。形容詞の最上級の前には定冠詞theが置かれることにも注意。よって、b. the most romantic（最もロマンチックな）が空欄に入る最も適切な選択肢となる。

4. The people in New York _____.
   - a. walks fast
   - b. walks fastly
   - c. walk fast
   - d. walk fastly

訳：ニューヨークの人びとは速く歩く。
解説：主語the peopleが複数なので、空欄に入る現在形の動詞に三単現-sは不必要。また、fastは「速く」という意味の副詞であることにも注意。

5. I have never met Chris and Pete's brother. Have you met _____?
   - a. them
   - b. he
   - c. they
   - d. him

訳：私はクリスとピートの兄（弟）に会ったことがありません。彼に会ったことがありますか？
解説：空欄にはChris and Pete's brotherの人称代名詞の目的格が入る。最も適切な形の人称代名詞はd. him（つまり、Chris and Pete's brother）である。

Lesson 4 (http://audio.lincenglish.com にアクセスして音声を聞いてください)

Part 1　Image Listening／写真描写問題

1. 左の写真を見て、人物の行動や物の位置などについて文を3つ作りなさい。

2. 写真の描写文として最も適切な文をA～Dの中から選びなさい。
   (A),　(B),　(C),　(D)

1. 左の写真を見て、人物の行動や物の位置などについて文を3つ作りなさい。

2. 写真の描写文として最も適切な文をA～Dの中から選びなさい。
   (A),　(B),　(C),　(D)

1. 左の写真を見て、人物の行動や物の位置などについて文を3つ作りなさい。

2. 写真の描写文として最も適切な文をA～Dの中から選びなさい。
   (A),　(B),　(C),　(D)

1. 左の写真を見て、人物の行動や物の位置などについて文を3つ作りなさい。

2. 写真の描写文として最も適切な文をA～Dの中から選びなさい。
   (A),　(B),　(C),　(D)

Part 2　Question and Response／質疑応答問題

重要な質問表現

Did you buy that coat at the mall?
　　「モールでそのコートを買ったかどうか」の事実に関する質問である。

Do you know how to get to Michael's house?
　　道順を知っているかの有無を尋ねている。

Look at my new iPod! Don't you love it?
　　don't you love it は、付加否定で始まっている同意を求める表現。

Do you speak any foreign languages?
　　話せる外国語を含めて応答する。

Where is the girl from?
　　出身を尋ねるお決まりのフレーズ。

Do you want to go to the river with me for a picnic?
　　ピクニックに行きたいかどうか。

How much time did it take to write your paper?
　　paper とは大学でよく使う、提出する「作文・論文」のこと。

Dad, can I please borrow the car?
　　can I please ～の please をいれることによってより丁寧な表現になる。

Why weren't you in class yesterday?
　　授業にいなかった「理由」をきかれている。

Where did Monica go after her important meeting?
　　時制は過去形で、モニカがミーティングの後どこに行ったかの質問文。

確認ドリル

次の1～5の質問に対して最も適切な応答をそれぞれ（A）～（C）の中から選びなさい。

1. Could you please help me make some spaghetti for dinner?
   (A)　Okay! Let's eat!
   (B)　Yes. I have eaten spaghetti before.
   (C)　Sure! How can I help you?

2. If I give you a camera, will you take a photograph of me?
   (A)　Of course! Smile!
   (B)　I didn't think so.
   (C)　You are smiling!

3. Listen! Can you hear that music inside the car?
   (A)　The car has a stereo.
   (B)　I have heard the music.
   (C)　I can hear it. It is country western music.

4. A "vegetarian" is a person who does not eat meat. Are you a vegetarian?
   (A)　Yes, I eat many vegetables.
   (B)　Yes, I eat meat.
   (C)　No, I am not a vegetarian. I love hamburgers!

5. Is it O.K. if I stay out late tonight?
   (A)　It's no problem.
   (B)　What's that?
   (C)　Me too!

Part 3 Short Conversation／会話問題

次の会話を読んで、質問に最も適当な答えを選びなさい。

> 質問文パターン

＊What 型パターン

1. **A**：Hi, Randy. Is that your new scooter?
   B：Yes, Julie, it is. It was on sale. Do you like it?
   A：The color is a little strange.

   Q：What does Julie think of Randy's scooter?
   a. She loves it.　　　　　　c. She doesn't like the color.
   b. She wants one like it.　　d. She has a scooter.

   解説：新しく買ったスクーターが話題になっている。

＊Why 型パターン

2. **A**：I am so excited! We are going to Hawaii next week!
   B：Why are you going there?
   A：I won a trip in a drawing contest.

   Q：Why is the person excited?
   a. Because he is going to be in a drawing contest.　　c. Because he is going to Hawaii.
   b. Because he is from Hawaii.　　　　　　　　　　　d. Because he won't get a vacation.

   解説：絵の大会賞品としてハワイ旅行が贈られた様子。

＊Where 型パターン

3. **A**：Tim said he is thinking about moving.
   B：Where does he want to move?
   A：Maybe somewhere where the weather is not so cold.

   Q：Where is Tim thinking of moving?
   a. To a warmer place.　　c. To a place where it snows.
   b. Somewhere cooler.　　d. To a colder place.

   解説：寒さが嫌いなようだ。

＊How 型パターン

4. **A**：I can't believe I have to work on Saturday!
   B：Yes, but it's because you took a vacation last week.
   A：Well, it's still not fair!

Q：How does he feel about working on Saturday?
  a. He is happy.　　c. He is glad.
  b. He is excited.　　d. He is upset.

解説：it's not fair「公平じゃない」と不満を漏らしている。

Part 4 Short Talks／説明文問題

次の説明文の質問に最も適当な答えを選びなさい。

ハワイ島

Hawaii was the last state to become part of the U.S. This wonderful group of islands became the 50th state on August 21, 1959. Hawaii is a beautiful land with beaches, jungles, waterfalls and many exotic animals. It produces large quantities of pineapple and sugar cane and has many active volcanoes. Almost 70% of the people who live in Hawaii are from Asian countries. Its biggest industry is tourism, with 7 million visitors every year. The Hawaiian word "aloha" means "hello", so Hawaii's nickname is the "Aloha State."

1. What is Hawaii's biggest industry?
    a. Volcanoes.   c. Vegetables.
    b. Fruit.   d. Tourism

2. What happened on August 21, 1959?
    a. Hawaii became the 50th state in the U.S.   c. Many people came to visit Hawaii.
    b. Hawaii's volcanoes erupted.   d. There was a big pineapple.

解説：設問1　sightseeing「観光」が一番盛んな事業。毎年 700 万人がハワイを訪れている。
　　　設問2　この日にハワイが 50 番目の州になりアメリカ合衆国の一部となった。

ファーマーズ・マーケット

Every Saturday in my hometown, there is a farmer's market. The farmer's market is a place where local farmers bring their fresh produce to sell to people. Some bring vegetables like cucumbers, tomatoes, carrots and onions. Others bring fresh flowers from their flower gardens in every color you can imagine. There is also a man who sells meat. Last week, I bought peaches, sunflowers and buffalo burger. I love to go to the farmer's market with my dad and watch all of the people.

1. What is one thing she bought last week?
    a. Cucumbers.   c. Buffalo burger.
    b. Onions.   d. Carrots.

2. What is a farmer's market?
    a. A place to cook food.   c. A place to have dinner.
    b. A place to buy fresh food.   d. A place to grow vegetables.

解説：設問1　文最後で先週買ったものが述べられている。バッファローは野生動物の一種である。
　　　設問2　文頭、The farmer's market is a place where local farmers bring their fresh produce to sell to people、つまり「新鮮な野菜を買える場所」である。

Part 5 Reading ／読解演習

次の段落文を読み、各設問に対して最も適切な答えを選びなさい（各段落速読問題は 2 分以内に終わらせなさい）。

スピードリーディング

Amelia Earhart is a famous woman in American history. In 1928, she flew across the Atlantic Ocean in an airplane. In 1932, she did something amazing. She became the first woman pilot to fly across the Atlantic Ocean by herself. In that same year, Ms. Earhart flew from New Jersey to California. She won many awards and was a wonderful pilot.

1. What ocean did Amelia fly across?
    a. The Atlantic.   c. The Indian.
    b. The Pacific.   d. The Arctic.

2. Where did Amelia fly in 1932?
    a. From the Atlantic to New Jersey.   c. From New Jersey to California.
    b. From California to New Jersey.   d. From Europe to the U.S.

When Amelia was a child, she asked many questions and was always interested in airplanes. When she was ten years old, she received a toy airplane as a Christmas gift. She loved the gift and kept it in her room for many years. Yet, she did not understand how an airplane could fly in the air. Amelia's interest as a child made her famous in American history.

1. When did Amelia receive a toy airplane?
    a. When she was a baby.   c. When she was a teenager.
    b. When she was eight.   d. When she was ten.

2. How long did she keep the gift in her room?
    a. For two years.   c. For many years.
    b. For eight years.   d. For a lifetime.

During her lifetime, Amelia had twenty-eight different jobs. She even had a job as a nurse in World War I. When she returned to the U.S., she was an English teacher and a social worker in Indiana. She gave lectures at universities, and many people respected her.

1. Where did Amelia teach English?
    a. In Indiana.   c. In an airplane.
    b. In India.   d. In World War I.

2. What did Amelia do at the universities?
    a. She studied English.   c. She gave lectures.
    b. She taught English.   d. She flew airplanes.

スピードリーディングと同じ文を読み、各設問に対して最も適切な答えを選びなさい。

読解問題

Amelia Earhart is a famous woman in American history. In 1928, she flew across the Atlantic Ocean in an airplane. In 1932, she did something amazing. She became the first woman pilot to fly across the Atlantic Ocean by herself. In that same year, Ms. Earhart flew from New Jersey to California. She won many awards and was a wonderful pilot.

When Amelia was a child, she asked many questions and was always interested in airplanes. When she was ten years old, she received a toy airplane as a Christmas gift. She loved the gift and kept it in her room for many years. Yet, she did not understand how an airplane could fly in the air. Amelia's interest as a child made her famous in American history.

During her lifetime, Amelia had twenty-eight different jobs. She even had a job as a nurse in World War I. When she returned to the U.S., she was an English teacher and a social worker in Indiana. She gave lectures at universities, and many people respected her.

She made her last flight on July 2nd at 12:30 p.m. with a friend. The weather started out good, but they soon flew into dark, cloudy skies and rain showers. People tried to call Earhart on her airplane radio, but the connection was very bad. People and search groups tried to find Ms. Earhart, but they were unsuccessful. On July 19th, they stopped looking for her. No one is truly sure how she died. People will remember Amelia for her skill, courage, and strong ideas.

Comprehension Questions

1. What was Amelia's occupation?
    a. A swimmer.   c. A saleswoman.
    b. A pilot.   d. An artist.

2. During what holiday did Amelia receive a toy airplane?
    a. Her birthday.   c. Christmas.
    b. When she was a child. d. When she was ten.

3. When did Amelia become an English teacher?
    a. On July 2nd.   c. After she was a nurse.
    b. Before she was a nurse. d. When she was twenty-eight.

4. How did Amelia die?
    a. She died in her sleep.   c. She had a car accident.
    b. She had an airplane accident. d. No one is sure how she died.

Part 6　Error Recognition／誤文訂正問題

各文には文法的誤りがあります。訂正もしくは書き換えを必要とする語句を選びなさい。

1. Bobby <u>hasn't seen</u> the new movie about <u>golfing</u>, and Emily <u>hasn't</u> <u>neither</u>.
 　　　　　A　　　　　　　　　　　　　　B　　　　　　　　　　C　　　D
 解説：not either：…も〜ない（注釈：neither A nor B：A と B 両方〜ない）
 正しい英文：Bobby hasn't seen the new movie about golfing, and Emily hasn't either.

2. <u>Some</u> Americans go out to eat at least five times a <u>week</u>. They <u>hardly</u> <u>never</u> cook at home.
 　　A　　　　　　　　　　　　　　　　　　　　　　　　　B　　　　　　C　　　D
 解説：hardly ever：めったに〜しない（副詞）
 正しい英文：Some Americans go out to eat at least five times a week. They hardly ever cook at home.

3. Rachel was lucky she <u>didn't break</u> her arm. She <u>could been</u> hurt <u>very</u> <u>badly</u>.
 　　　　　　　　　　　　　A　　　　　　　　　　　　　B　　　　　C　　　D
 解説：could have ＋過去分詞：〜していただろう（実際にはしなかった）
 正しい英文：Rachel was lucky she didn't break her arm. She could have been hurt very badly.

4. I <u>have</u> a lot of homework. It <u>will take</u> five hours <u>probably</u> <u>to complete</u>.
 　　A　　　　　　　　　　　　　　B　　　　　　　　　　C　　　　　　D
 解説：2 文目において、副詞 probably の置かれている位置が誤り。通例、副詞は助動詞の後に置かれる。
 　　　 よって、正しい語順は will probably take となる。
 正しい英文：I have a lot of homework. It will probably take five hours to complete.

5. My mother writes <u>more</u> <u>careful</u> <u>than</u> my little brother. His handwriting is <u>terrible</u>.
 　　　　　　　　　　　　A　　B　　 C　　　　　　　　　　　　　　　　　　　D
 解説：意味内容的に、下線 B には副詞 carefully（慎重に）が適切である。訳参照。
 正しい英文：My mother writes more carefully than my little brother. His handwriting is terrible.

6. I <u>have heard</u> that rock band <u>before</u>. They play <u>loud</u>, and their music isn't that <u>great</u>.
 　　　A　　　　　　　　　　　B　　　　　　　　　C　　　　　　　　　　　　　　D
 解説：意味内容的に、2 文目の形容詞 loud は副詞 loudly（（音が）大きく）であることが適切である。訳参照。
 正しい英文：I have heard that rock band before. They play loudly, and their music isn't that great.

7. I think <u>I'm</u> going to order <u>a</u> black bean soup for an appetizer. What are you <u>going</u> <u>to order</u>?
 　　　　　A　　　　　　　　　B　　　　　　　　　　　　　　　　　　　　　　　C　　 D
 解説：名詞 soup は不可算名詞であることから、不定冠詞 a がその前に置かれることは不可となる。
 正しい英文：I think I'm going to order the black bean soup for an appetizer. What are you going to order?

Part 7　Incomplete Sentence／文法・語彙問題

文法的に適切な語句を1つ選び、文を完成させなさい。

1. I don't like broccoli. I don't like carrots _____ .
    - a. neither
    - b. either
    - c. both
    - d. with

    訳：私はブロッコリーが好きではない。にんじんも好きではない。
    解説：either は「〜も…ない」という「否定」をさらに重ねるときに用いられる副詞である（注釈：「肯定」をさらに重ねるときに用いられる副詞は too や also などが使われる）。

2. Please don't wear shoes in my house. _____ outside.
    - a. Them take off
    - b. Take them off
    - c. It take off
    - d. Take it off

    訳：私の家の中で靴を履かないでください。そとで靴を脱いでください。
    解説：take O off（take off O）：（服・靴など）を脱ぐ shoes（靴）は複数であることにも注意。よって、名詞 shoes の目的格代名詞は them となる。

3. I love Lisa's new purse. Where _____ ?
    - a. she did buy it
    - b. did she buy it
    - c. it she buy
    - d. did it she buy

    訳：私はリサの新しい財布を気に入っている。彼女はどこでそれを買ったの？
    解説：文法的に、b. did she buy it が空欄に入る最も適切な語である。2文目は疑問文なので、空欄には助動詞（ここでは did）が主語（ここでは she）の前に倒置されることに注意。

4. Dennis _____ his finger several times with that knife.
    - a. cutted
    - b. has cutted
    - c. cut
    - d. has cut

    訳：デニスはあのナイフで自分の指を何回か切っている。
    解説：副詞句 several times（何度か）があることから、ここでは「経験」の意味を表す現在完了形が空欄に入る適切な動詞句である。よって、正しい現在完了形は d. has cut。cut（現在）- cut（過去）- cut（過去分詞）

5. Kevin was fishing _____ Angela was swimming.
    - a. during
    - b. also
    - c. while
    - d. until

    訳：アンジェラが泳いでいる間、ケビンは魚釣りをしていた。
    解説：空欄以下は節が続いているため、接続詞 c. while（〜の間）が空欄に入る最も適切な語である。d. until（〜まで）も接続詞だが、ここでは意味内容的に不可となる。

Lesson 5 （http://audio.lincenglish.com にアクセスして音声を聞いてください）

Part 1　Image Listening ／写真描写問題

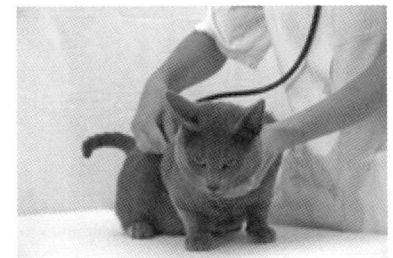

1. 左の写真を見て、人物の行動や物の位置などについて文を3つ作りなさい。
   _____
   _____

2. 写真の描写文として最も適切な文をA～Dの中から選びなさい。
   （A），（B），（C），（D）

1. 左の写真を見て、人物の行動や物の位置などについて文を3つ作りなさい。
   _____
   _____

2. 写真の描写文として最も適切な文をA～Dの中から選びなさい。
   （A），（B），（C），（D）

1. 左の写真を見て、人物の行動や物の位置などについて文を3つ作りなさい。
   _____
   _____

2. 写真の描写文として最も適切な文をA～Dの中から選びなさい。
   （A），（B），（C），（D）

1. 左の写真を見て、人物の行動や物の位置などについて文を3つ作りなさい。
   _____
   _____

2. 写真の描写文として最も適切な文をA～Dの中から選びなさい。
   （A），（B），（C），（D）

Part 2 Question and Response／質疑応答問題

重要な質問表現

How much money is in the jar?
　「つぼ」の中に入っている金額をきかれている。

Do you like your new apartment?
　「アパートが好きか」どうかについての質問。

What does your teacher look like?
　look like「〜のように見える」。

How are your hunting skills?
　how「どのように」ときかれているので、goodやbadなどを使って具体的に表現する。

How much does that bag of cherries weigh?
　weighは動詞で「重さがある」。weightは名詞で「体重」としても使われる。

Why did you throw your test away?
　throw away「捨てる」。

Does anyone know where my keys are?
　鍵を探している。

Do you have any roommates?
　roommateとは住んでいる場所を一緒に共有する人のことを指す。アメリカでは一般的である。

How long have you been a student here?
　生徒でいる期間を答える。

What do you want on your pizza?
　「ピザに何が欲しい」、つまりは「何をピザにのせたいか」である。

確認ドリル

次の1〜5の質問に対して最も適切な応答をそれぞれ（A）〜（C）の中から選びなさい。

1. When will you know if you got the job or not?
　(A)　In a few weeks.
　(B)　The job is in Milan.
　(C)　She will get the job.

2. Have you been waiting for a long time?
　(A)　Yes, she does.
　(B)　Yes, it is.
　(C)　Yes, I have.

3. How long will it take to drive to Seattle?
　(A)　It's about time!
　(B)　About ten hours.
　(C)　How about tomorrow?

4. Do you want to go to the park with me?
　(A)　Yes, it couldn't be better.
　(B)　Yes, I would love to.
　(C)　We're almost there.

5. Isn't the sunset beautiful?
　(A)　I am so beautiful.
　(B)　It is lovely.
　(C)　The sun is shining.

Part 3 Short Conversation／会話問題

次の会話を読んで、質問に最も適当な答えを選びなさい。

質問文パターン

* Why 型パターン

1. **A**：We really need a new microwave.
    B：I heard that there is a sale this week at the total Home store.
    A：Really? We should go there right away before the microwaves are sold out.

    Q：Why does the woman want to go to the Total Home store right away?
    　　a. Because the store is across town.　　c. Because the microwaves might sell out soon.
    　　b. Because the store does not　　　　d. Because the Total Home store sells
    　　　　have microwaves.　　　　　　　　　　many things.

    解説：電子レンジは microwave という。言い方が違うので覚えておこう。

* Who 型パターン

2. **A**：Mr. Hansen, I'd like to introduce you to our new sales manager, Ms. Thomas.
    B：It's very nice to meet you, Ms. Thomas.
    A：Ms. Thomas will be taking Mr. James' place when he retires next week.

    Q：Who will retire soon?
    　　a. Mr. Hansen.　　c. Mr. James.
    　　b. Ms. Thomas.　　d. No one.

    解説：take one's place「(人の) ポジション・位をとる」。

* Where 型パターン

3. **A**：Steven, do you have the concert tickets?
    B：No, I gave them to Kate, and she left them at Mary's house.
    A：O.K. I will call her and ask her to go get them.

    Q：Where are the concert tickets?
    　　a. Steven has them.　　　　　　c. They are at Mary's house.
    　　b. Kate has them with her.　　d. They are at Kate's house.

    解説：コンサートのチケットはメアリーに属している。

* What 型パターン

4. **A**：Thank you so much for helping me move to my new apartment!
    B：No problem. Anything to help out a friend.
    A：Well, I really appreciate it. Can I buy you dinner?

Q：What would she like to do for her friend?
  a. Make him dinner. c. Help him move.
  b. Buy him dinner. d. Find him a new friend.

解説：help out（人）で「〜を手助けする」。

Part 4 Short Talks ／説明文問題

次の説明文の質問に最も適当な答えを選びなさい。

芸術家ジャーミー

Jeremy is an artist from a big family of artists. His mother likes to paint beautiful pictures of horses. His father makes sculptures of people out of clay. When Jeremy was a child, he picked up his first paint set and painted a picture of the sky. His painting was so good that his teacher put it in a contest for young artists. He won first place in the contest, and he won a trip to California. The contest even put his painting on a calendar. Today, Jeremy is a student at the university. His major is, of course, art.

1. What did Jeremy's teacher do with his painting?
   - a. Put it on the cover of a book.
   - b. Put it in a contest.
   - c. Put it on the wall.
   - d. Put it in the garbage can.

2. What does his mother like to paint?
   - a. Pictures of California.
   - b. Pictures of Jeremy.
   - c. Pictures of horses.
   - d. Pictures of people.

解説：設問1　ジャーミーが子どものときに初めての色彩セットで描いた絵を先生が気に入り、コンテストに出品した。

設問2　文頭、母親は馬の絵を描くのが好きな画家で、父親は彫刻家のようだ。

色と感情

Some people associate colors with feelings or emotions. In American culture, the color black is often associated with death or negative things, whereas white is a symbol of purity. People often think of yellow as a happy color, and red is associated with power. Good luck is represented by the color green, and purple is the color of royalty. Blue is calm and peaceful. Of course, each culture has its own general feeling about colors, and each person has his or her own opinion. For example, in some cultures red is considered good luck, not green.

1. According to the speaker, what color is often associated with happiness?
   - a. Green.
   - b. Blue.
   - c. Yellow.
   - d. White.

2. Do all cultures associate good luck with the color green?
   - a. Yes, green means good luck in every culture.
   - b. No, every culture considers red to be good luck.
   - c. Yes, all cultures agree on certain feelings associated with colors.
   - d. No, every culture has a different opinion.

解説：設問1　語り手によると幸福は緑色だが、違う文化では赤が幸運とされているらしい。混乱しないようにしよう。

設問2　緑にかかわらず、それぞれの文化によって色の意味は異なる。

Part 5　Reading ／読解演習

次の段落文を読み、各設問に対して最も適切な答えを選びなさい（各段落速読問題は2分以内に終わらせなさい）。

スピードリーディング

　In 1850, Levi Strauss moved to San Francisco. He was an immigrant from Germany. At this time, thousands of people were moving to California to dig for gold. The people who worked and looked for the gold were called miners. Levi did not look for gold; he sold canvas to the gold miners. Canvas is heavy material and very strong.

1. Where did Levi move from?
    a. San Francisco.　　c. Germany.
    b. California.　　d. Japan.

2. People who look for gold are called what?
    a. Californians.　　c. Majors.
    b. Miners.　　d. Workers.

　The miners worked all day outside, and their clothes were very dirty. They complained because their clothes were not very good. Levi had an idea. He took the canvas material and made pants. In one day Levi sold all of the pants to the miners.

1. Why did the miners complain?
    a. Because the weather was cold.　　c. Because their arms were tired.
    b. Because they did not find gold.　　d. Because their clothes were not good.

2. What did Levi make from the canvas material?
    a. Shirts.　　c. Pants.
    b. An idea.　　d. Miners.

　Levi wanted to make the pants look and feel better. He found softer material than canvas but that was as strong as canvas. He bought the fabric from France, and it was known as denim. Levi sold many denim pants to the miners after a month.

1. Where did Levi buy the material?
    a. The U.S.　　c. California.
    b. France.　　d. Spain.

2. What kind of material did Levi buy?
    a. Heavy, dark material.　　c. Light, strong material.
    b. Soft, strong material.　　d. Small, heavy material.

スピードリーディングと同じ文を読み、各設問に対して最も適切な答えを選びなさい。

読解問題

In 1850, Levi Strauss moved to San Francisco. He was an immigrant from Germany. At this time, thousands of people were moving to California to dig for gold. The people who worked and looked for the gold were called miners. Levi did not look for gold; he sold canvas to the gold miners. Canvas is heavy material and very strong.

The miners worked all day outside, and their clothes were very dirty. They complained because their clothes were not very good. Levi had an idea. He took the canvas material and made pants. In one day Levi sold all of the pants to the miners.

Levi wanted to make the pants look and feel better. He found softer material than canvas but that was as strong as canvas. He bought the fabric from France, and it was known as denim. Levi sold many denim pants to the miners after a month.

However, Levi wanted to make the pants even better. The denim was not pretty and the pants got very dirty. Levi dyed the denim blue. His new pants were a huge success. Today, the Levi Strauss Company is known around the world and is very popular. People used to wear denim jeans for work, but now they are very fashionable.

The miners got rich from the gold, and Levi got rich from his pants!

Comprehension Questions

1. What did Levi first sell to the miners?
    a. Gold.   c. Softer material.
    b. Canvas.   d. Pants.

2. In how many days did Levi sell his pants?
    a. One day.   c. Two weeks.
    b. 82 days.   d. One week.

3. How long did Levi have to wait for the denim?
    a. One day.   c. One month.
    b. One week. d. One year.

4. Why did Levi want to make the pants even better?
    a. Because the pants were heavy.   c. Because the pants were fashionable.
    b. Because the pants were blue.   d. Because the pants were ugly.

Part 6 Error Recognition ／誤文訂正問題

各文には文法的誤りがあります。訂正もしくは書き換えを必要とする語句を選びなさい。

1. The answers to the test <u>was</u> very easy. I <u>studied</u> for <u>several</u> hours, and I <u>have studied</u> the information before.
   　　　　　　　　　　　　　 A　　　　　　　　　B　　　　　　 C　　　　　　　　　　 D

   解説：1文目の主語 the answers が複数形であることから、下線Aのbe動詞は were が適切である。

   正しい英文：The answers to the test were very easy. I studied for several hours, and I have studied the information before.

2. You'll <u>feel</u> guilty if you <u>aren't returning</u> the diamond ring. Give it back to the owner, so <u>you'll stop</u> talking
   　　　　 A　　　　　　　　　 B　　　　　　　　　　　　　　　　　　　　　　　　　　　　　　　　　　　　　 C
   about <u>it</u>.
   　　　　 D

   解説：if 節内では、通例、現在形（未来の事柄を表す）か過去形（物事の仮定を表す）が用いられる。

   正しい英文：You'll feel guilty if you don't return the diamond ring. Give it back to the owner, so you'll stop talking about it.

3. Never <u>talk</u> to a stranger. More <u>important</u>, never get into a <u>stranger's</u> car even if he or she looks like a nice,
   　　　　 A　　　　　　　　　　　　　　　 B　　　　　　　　　　　　　　 C
   <u>friendly</u> person.
   　 D

   解説：more importantly：さらに重要なことに（副詞）。訳参照。

   正しい英文：Never talk to a stranger. More importantly, never get into a stranger's car even if he or she looks like a nice, friendly person.

4. My mother and my aunt are the same <u>tall</u>. However, my aunt is <u>much</u> older than my mother. My aunt
   　　　　　　　　　　　　　　　　　　　　　 A　　　　　　　　　　　　　 B
   <u>was born</u> in 1938, and my mother was born ten years <u>later</u>.
   　 C　　　　　　　　　　　　　　　　　　　　　　　　　　　　　 D

   解説：A and B are the same height：AとBは同じ背の高さ（＝A is as tall as B）

   正しい英文：My mother and my aunt are the same height. However, my aunt is much older than my mother. My aunt was born in 1938, and my mother was born ten years later.

5. Dogs are much <u>happier</u> animals than cats. In addition, they <u>haven't</u> the rude personality <u>that</u> cats <u>have</u>.
   　　　　　　　　　 A　　　　　　　　　　　　　　　　　　　　　　 B　　　　　　　　　　　　　　　 C　　　　 D

   解説：下線Bは文法的に誤りである。動詞 have を否定形にするときは do（does）not have となる。

   正しい英文：Dogs are much happier animals than cats. In addition, they don't have the rude personality that cats have.

6. I read the previous chapter <u>which</u> <u>to understand</u> the information. Otherwise, it would <u>have been</u> too <u>difficult</u>.
　　　　　　　　　　　　　　　　A　　　　　B　　　　　　　　　　　　　　　　　　　C　　　　　　　D

　　解説：in order to do：〜するために

　　正しい英文：I read the previous chapter in order to understand the information. Otherwise, it would have been too difficult.

7. Dan slept <u>badly</u> last night <u>although</u> he <u>stayed up</u> to watch two movies. He looks very <u>tired</u>.
　　　　　　　A　　　　　　　　B　　　　　　C　　　　　　　　　　　　　　　　　　　　　　　　D

　　解説：文脈から、接続詞 because（なぜなら）が下線 B に置かれる適切な語である。訳参照。

　　正しい英文：Dan slept badly last night because he stayed up to watch two movies. He looks very tired.

Part 7 Incomplete Sentence ／文法・語彙問題

文法的に適切な語句を1つ選び、文を完成させなさい。

1. The teacher always asks the students _____ they spend studying for tests.
   - a. how many time
   - b. how much time
   - c. how many times
   - d. how often

訳：その先生はいつも生徒にテストにどのくらいの時間を費やすかを尋ねる。
解説：ここでは time（時間）の「量」について述べられているため、b. how much time が空欄に入る最も適切な語となる（注釈：How many times は「回数」を尋ねるときに用いられる疑問詞句。例：How many times have you been to Japan?：日本へ何回行ったことがありますか？）。

2. You are from Scotland, _____?
   - a. are you
   - b. aren't you
   - c. can you
   - d. can't you

訳：スコットランド出身ですよね？
解説：付加疑問文（ですよね？）は肯定文では否定文、否定文では肯定文が用いられる。You don't like vegetables, do you?：野菜が好きじゃないんですよね。

3. I _____ Denise yesterday. She just bought a puppy.
   - a. seen
   - b. saw
   - c. have seen
   - d. was seeing

訳：昨日デニスを見た。彼女は子犬を買ったばかりだ。
解説：文中に、過去の事柄を表す副詞 yesterday があるため、空欄には過去形の動詞が適切である。よって、b. saw が空欄に入る最も適切な語となる。

4. Matt hasn't decided yet, but _____ about moving to Tokyo.
   - a. thinks
   - b. he is thinking
   - c. he had thinking
   - d. did thought

訳：まだ決めていないが、マットは東京に引っ越すことを考えている。
解説：文法的に適切な語は、現在進行形（be 動詞＋-ing）の b. he is thinking である。

5. That is Melissa's cell phone. Please _____.
   - a. give it her
   - b. giving it to her
   - c. give it to her
   - d. give she the phone

訳：あれはメリッサの携帯電話です。彼女に渡してください。
解説：give O1 to O2（＝give O2 O1）：O2 に O1 を与える。

Lesson 6 （http://audio.lincenglish.com にアクセスして音声を聞いてください）

Part 1　Image Listening／写真描写問題

1. 左の写真を見て、人物の行動や物の位置などについて文を3つ作りなさい。
   _____
   _____

2. 写真の描写文として最も適切な文をA〜Dの中から選びなさい。
   （A），（B），（C），（D）

1. 左の写真を見て、人物の行動や物の位置などについて文を3つ作りなさい。
   _____
   _____

2. 写真の描写文として最も適切な文をA〜Dの中から選びなさい。
   （A），（B），（C），（D）

1. 左の写真を見て、人物の行動や物の位置などについて文を3つ作りなさい。
   _____
   _____

2. 写真の描写文として最も適切な文をA〜Dの中から選びなさい。
   （A），（B），（C），（D）

1. 左の写真を見て、人物の行動や物の位置などについて文を3つ作りなさい。
   _____
   _____

2. 写真の描写文として最も適切な文をA〜Dの中から選びなさい。
   （A），（B），（C），（D）

Part 2　Question and Response／質疑応答問題

重要な質問表現

How old is your best friend?
　　きかれているのは「親友」の「年齢」である。

Who cares?
　　who cares?「誰が気にするか（誰も気にしない）」。

What do you recommend from the menu?
　　お勧めのメニューを答える。

Where does this bowl go?
　　ボウルを置くべき「位置」はどこか。

How do you know Brian?
　　どのようにブライアンを知っているかの質問。

How much should I leave the waitress as a tip?
　　tip「チップ」は担当してくれたウェイトレスに合計金額の 10 ～ 20％ 相当をサービス料として与えるものである。アメリカの大事なマナーの 1 つとされている。

How did your test go?
　　how から始まる疑問文には具体的な様子を含んだ応答をする。

Would you like a ride to work?
　　a ride は名詞で「車にのること」となる。

You like chocolate, don't you?
　　チョコレートが好きだという事実を確認している。

Will that be everything?
　　will that be everything?「それで全部ですか？」は is that all for you?「これがあなたにとって全部ですか？」等と同じように、店のレジなどでよく店員に聞かれるフレーズである。覚えておこう。

確認ドリル

次の 1 ～ 5 の質問に対して最も適切な応答をそれぞれ (A) ～ (C) の中から選びなさい。

1. What seems to be the problem?
   (A)　I lost my phone.
   (B)　Of course!
   (C)　I don't think it's possible.

2. What did your teacher say about your final grade?
   (A)　She said I did a good job in her class.
   (B)　She said yes.
   (C)　She's a great teacher.

3. Do you know why Seth left early?
   (A)　He didn't come on time.
   (B)　He wasn't feeling well.
   (C)　You're kidding!

4. Whose turn is it?
   (A)　She said no.
   (B)　Nathan is next.
   (C)　I'm afraid not.

5. Does he like to play video games?
   (A)　He's crazy about them.
   (B)　He's crazy.
   (C)　I played a video game last night.

Part 3　Short Conversation／会話問題

次の会話を読んで、質問に最も適当な答えを選びなさい。

質問文パターン

* Where 型パターン

1. **A**：It looks like you got a new car. When did you buy that?
   B：It's a graduation present from my grandfather. What do you think?
   A：It's awesome! Can we go for a ride?

   Q：Where did he get the car?
   　　a. From the car dealer.　　c. From his friend.
   　　b. From his grandfather.　　d. From his teacher when he graduated.

   解説：卒業祝いに祖父から新しい車を買ってもらった。

* Which 型パターン

2. **A**：Which bike do you like more, the blue one or the green one?
   B：Actually, my favorite is the purple bike, Dad.
   A：Oh, I didn't know you like the color purple. I'll buy that one for you.

   Q：Which bike will his father buy him?
   　　a. The blue bike.　　c. The purple bike.
   　　b. The green bike.　　d. None of them.

   解説：父親は息子が好きな色を知らなかった。

* Why 型パターン

3. **A**：This plant grows beautiful pink flowers in the summertime.
   B：What is the name of the plant?
   A：It's called a lipstick plant because the flowers are shaped like tubes of lipstick.

   Q：Why is the plant called a lipstick plant?
   　　a. Because the plant smells　　c. Because the flowers grow in the summertime.
   　　　　like makeup.
   　　b. Because you can use the flowers　　d. Because the flowers are shaped like tubes
   　　　　as makeup.　　　　　　　　　　　　　of lipstick.

   解説：shape「形づくる」。

* What 型パターン

4. **A**：Do you know how to make chili, Penny?

   B：Actually, my mother taught me how to make it when I was a little girl.

   A：My mother taught me how to make meatloaf.

   Q：What did Penny's mother teach her to make?
   - a. Meatloaf.
   - b. Chili.
   - c. Pie.
   - d. Breakfast.

解説：ペニーの母親はチリを、もう片方のスピーカーの母親はミートローフの作り方を伝授した。ペニーがどちらのスピーカーなのか判断することが大事である。

Part 4　Short Talks／説明文問題

次の説明文の質問に最も適当な答えを選びなさい。

ハイキング

Have you ever gone hiking? I love to go outside in the summertime and go for a hike. I walk up in the mountains and smell the fresh air. There are many flowers and plants, and you can hear the birds singing in the trees. One time I even saw a deer! When he heard me coming, he ran away. Hiking is great because spending time in nature makes me feel relaxed.

1. How does spending time in nature make him feel?
    a. Excited.　　c. Nervous.
    b. Relaxed.　　d. Bored.

2. What does he hear when he goes hiking?
    a. Deer eating.　　c. Birds singing.
    b. People talking.　　d. Water moving.

解説：設問1　makes me feel relaxed とハイキングをすることで「気分が落ち着く」らしい。
　　　設問2　山を歩くと、鳥のさえずりが聞こえてくる。

エルブス・プレスリー博物館

Welcome to the Elvis Presley Museum. Admission is $10 for adults and $5 for children and people over 50 years old. In the museum you can see Elvis' guitar, his gold records, and the suit he wore at his last concert. We play his music all day, and if you want, you can have a peanut butter and banana sandwich, which was his favorite food. Come early, because the museum is very busy after 11:00 a.m. We open at 9:00 a.m. If you love Elvis, you will love this museum!

1. What time does the museum open?
    a. 11:00 a.m.　　c. 9:00 a.m.
    b. 11:00 p.m.　　d. 10:00 a.m.

2. What was Elvis' favorite food?
    a. Pizza.　　　　　　　　　　　　　　c. A ham sandwich.
    b. A peanut butter and banana sandwich.　　d. A tuna sandwich.

解説：設問1　文の最後に開館は午前9時とある。
　　　設問2　この博物館では実際にエルビスの好物だった、ピーナッツバターとバナナのサンドウィッチを食べることができる。

Part 5 Reading／読解演習

次の段落文を読み、各設問に対して最も適切な答えを選びなさい（各段落速読問題は2分以内に終わらせなさい）。

スピードリーディング

　America loves entertainment. Entertainment is an activity that people enjoy doing or seeing. For example, concerts, movies, museums, plays, and basketball games are types of popular entertainment in the U.S. In large cities, such as New York City, entertainment never stops. Specifically, people love to see and create music. Jazz, a type of music, was first created in the United States. It is the only type of music created in the United States.

    1. What do Americans specifically love to see and create?
        a. Books.   c. Entertainment.
        b. Music.   d. Sports.

    2. What kind of music was first created in the United States?
        a. Hip-hop.   c. Concerts.
        b. Country.   d. Jazz.

　Jazz was created by black Americans. Many blacks had to come from Africa to America as slaves. A slave is a person who does not have freedom and who must obey the head of the house. Many slaves had to leave their families in Africa. As a way to forget about the pain, the black slaves sang and played the music of their homeland.

    1. Who created jazz?
        a. North Americans.   c. White Americans.
        b. Black Americans.   d. Europeans.

    2. What is a slave?
        a. A person who has no freedom.   c. A person from Africa.
        b. A person who makes music.   d. A person who likes music.

　Jazz is a combination of many different kinds of music. Many slaves sang about the hard work, and others sang about religion. Many times, the jazz singers did not have written words, so they thought of words quickly. They sang from the heart. A jazz song might sound a little different each time it is played.

    1. Where did the singers get the words for the songs?
        a. On a piece of paper.   c. In a book.
        b. From their families.   d. From their hearts.

    2. What could happen every time people sang jazz?
        a. The song may change.   c. The singers drink some water.
        b. It may make people sad.   d. The singers get tired.

スピードリーディングと同じ文を読み、各設問に対して最も適切な答えを選びなさい。

読解問題

America loves entertainment. Entertainment is an activity that people enjoy doing or seeing. For example, concerts, movies, museums, plays, and basketball games are types of popular entertainment in the U.S. In large cities, such as New York City, entertainment never stops. Specifically, people love to see and create music. Jazz, a type of music, was first created in the United States. It is the only type of music created in the United States.

Jazz was created by black Americans. Many blacks had to come from Africa to America as slaves. A slave is a person who does not have freedom and who must obey the head of the house. Many slaves had to leave their families in Africa. As a way to forget about the pain, the black slaves sang and played the music of their homeland.

Jazz is a combination of many different kinds of music. Many slaves sang about the hard work, and others sang about religion. Many times, the jazz singers did not have written words, so they thought of words quickly. They sang from the heart. A jazz song might sound a little different each time it is played.

In the early 1800s, jazz was only played with a small group of black slaves, often in secret. In the late 1800s, jazz bands began to form. The black Americans played in bars and clubs in the large cities. It was especially popular in the southern city called New Orleans. In the early 1900s, people from all over the U.S. began listening to the powerful words and the loud instruments of jazz. Today, jazz music is still very popular.

Comprehension Questions

1. When does entertainment stop in New York City?
    a. At 2:00 a.m.   c. Never.
    b. At midnight.   d. Always.

2. Why did many slaves play music?
    a. To become good musicians.   c. To earn money.
    b. To be good to the head of the house. d. To forget about the difficult times.

3. Why might a jazz song sound different every time?
    a. Because there are new singers.   c. Because the music might not be loud.
    b. Because the singers do not always   d. Because the people play in different cities.
       have written words.

4. When did Americans from northern, western, and eastern areas begin listening to jazz?
    a. In the early 1900s.   c. In 1889.
    b. Before the 1800s.   d. In the early 1800s.

Part 6 Error Recognition／誤文訂正問題

各文には文法的誤りがあります。訂正もしくは書き換えを必要とする語句を選びなさい。

1. Sylvia hardly never eats meat. In fact, she's probably a vegetarian. What do you think?
   　　　　　　　A　　　　　　　　　　　　　　B　　C　　　　　　　　　　　D

   解説：hardly ever：滅多に～ない

   正しい英文：Sylvia hardly ever eats meat. In fact, she's probably a vegetarian. What do you think?

2. Randy and Kevin are great friends. They have known themselves for years. They are also neighbors.
   　　　　　　　　　A　　　　　　　　　　　B　　　　　C　　　　　　　　　　　　D

   解説：each other は2人の人に用いられる再帰代名詞（主語の代名詞）である。know each other：互いを知る

   正しい英文：Randy and Kevin are great friends. They have known each other for years. They are also neighbors.

3. Carmen is very self-centered. She always looks at hers in the mirror. Every day before class, she puts on
   　　　　　　　　　　　　　　　　　　　A　　　B　　　　　　　　　　　　　　　　　　　　　　C
   too much makeup.
   　　　D

   解説：再帰代名詞 herself（彼女自身）が下線Bに適した語である。

   正しい英文：Carmen is very self-centered. She always looks at herself in the mirror. Every day before class, she puts on too much makeup.

4. I've got Bill's keys in my pocket. I must give back them to him. I'll see him tomorrow.
   　　　　　A　　　　　　　　　　　　　　　　　B　　　　　　C　　D

   解説：give O1 back to O2：O1をO2に返す（＝give O2 back O1）

   正しい英文：I've got Bill's keys in my pocket. I must give them back to him. I'll see him tomorrow.

5. The plane took out twenty minutes late. Now, Jerry's arrival time is 6:20, not 6:00. He might miss the
   　　　　　　A　　　　　　　　　　　　　　　　　　　B
   important meeting with the boss.
   　　C　　　　　　　D

   解説：1文目の主語が the plane（飛行機）であることから、take off（離陸する）が下線Aに置かれる適切な動詞句である。

   正しい英文：The plane took off twenty minutes late. Now, Jerry's arrival time is 6:20, not 6:00. He might miss the important meeting with the boss.

6. It's getting late. I need going now. I'm supposed to be at the doctor's office at 9:00. I should hurry.
   　　　　A　　　　　　B　　　　　　　　　　C　　　　　　　　　　　　　　　　　　　　　D

   解説：need to do：～する必要がある

   正しい英文：It's getting late. I need to go now. I'm supposed to be at the doctor's office at 9:00. I should hurry.

7. I hate <u>rush</u> hour. There are <u>too enough</u> cars in the street. Next time, I'm going <u>to leave</u> work <u>earlier</u>.
           A   B   C   D

解説：下線 B には too many（多すぎる）が適切である。too enough という表現は無い。

正しい英文：I hate rush hour. There are too many cars in the street. Next time, I'm going to leave work earlier.

Part 7　Incomplete Sentence ／文法・語彙問題

文法的に適切な語句を1つ選び、文を完成させなさい。

1. My brother _____ German for the past two years. He wants to study in Munich next year.
   　　　　a. has been practicing　　c. will practice
   　　　　b. practiced　　　　　　　d. has never practiced

   訳：私の兄（弟）は過去2年間、ドイツ語を練習している。彼は来年、ミュンヘンで勉強したがっている。
   解説：「期間」を表す副詞句 for the past two years.（過去2年間）に注意しよう。よって、事柄の「継続」を表す現在完了進行形 a. has been practicing が空欄に入る適切な語となる。問2参照。

2. Currently, scientists _____ ways to cure cancer.
   　　　　a. find　　　　c. have found
   　　　　b. are finding　d. finding

   訳：現在、科学者はガンを治療する方法を見つけている。
   解説：副詞 currently（現在）が文頭に置かれているため、現在行われている事柄を表すため、現在進行形（be動詞＋-ing）が空欄に入る最も適切な動詞句だと推測できる。

3. I _____ Heather to know the answer, but she didn't.
   　　　　a. expected　　　c. thought
   　　　　b. had expected　d. had thought

   訳：ヘザーが答えを知っていると思っていたが、彼女は知らなかった。
   解説：but 以下の時制が過去形であることから、文全体において、過去の事柄が述べられていると推測できる。よって、空欄には過去形動詞 a. expected（～を期待する）が入る。expect O to do：O が～するだろうと思う

4. If you think you know the answer, _____ your hand.
   　　　　a. then raise　　c. then will raise
   　　　　b. than raise　　d. than will raise

   訳：答えが分かったと思ったら、手を上げなさい。
   解説：if と then はしばしば呼応して用いられるので注意しよう。意味内容的に、（コンマ）以下の文が命令文になっていることが自然である。よって、空欄には、a. then raise が適切。訳参照。

5. I don't need _____. I can do it alone.
   　　　　a. any help　　c. no help
   　　　　b. a help　　　d. little help

   訳：助けはいりません。1人でできます。
   解説：否定語 not と any はしばしば呼応して使われるので注意。not と any で完全否定（＝no）を表す。例：I don't have any money on me：お金をまったく持っていません（＝ I have no money.）。

Lesson 7 (http://audio.lincenglish.com にアクセスして音声を聞いてください)

Part 1　Image Listening／写真描写問題

1. 左の写真を見て、人物の行動や物の位置などについて文を3つ作りなさい。
   _____
   _____
   _____

2. 写真の描写文として最も適切な文をA～Dの中から選びなさい。
   (A),　(B),　(C),　(D)

1. 左の写真を見て、人物の行動や物の位置などについて文を3つ作りなさい。
   _____
   _____
   _____

2. 写真の描写文として最も適切な文をA～Dの中から選びなさい。
   (A),　(B),　(C),　(D)

1. 左の写真を見て、人物の行動や物の位置などについて文を3つ作りなさい。
   _____
   _____
   _____

2. 写真の描写文として最も適切な文をA～Dの中から選びなさい。
   (A),　(B),　(C),　(D)

1. 左の写真を見て、人物の行動や物の位置などについて文を3つ作りなさい。
   _____
   _____
   _____

2. 写真の描写文として最も適切な文をA～Dの中から選びなさい。
   (A),　(B),　(C),　(D)

Part 2　Question and Response／質疑応答問題

重要な質問表現

How did she do on the test?
　　how did you do on the test? は試験後に出来具合を聞く表現としてよく使われるのでそのまま覚えておこう。
How do you know Tara?
　　how do you know ～「どうやって～を知っているのか」。
Did you gamble at the horse race?
　　gamble「賭けをする」。
Did the teacher tell you when the homework is due?
　　due「締切り」。
Did you finish washing the dishes?
　　動作についての質問。
Can you believe the size of that truck?
　　トラックの大きさについて何やら同意を求めているようだ。
When will that stereo be on sale?
　　問題文は、単純に「いつ」と日時をきいている。
How come?
　　how come は why と同じ意味をもつ。
Do you like my new earrings?
　　新しいイヤリングについて意見を求められている。
How many times have you gone skiing?
　　has been to「～に行ったことがある」。ちなみに has gone to「～に行ってしまった（今いない状態）」との違いを再確認しておこう。

確認ドリル

次の1～5の質問に対して最も適切な応答をそれぞれ (A)～(C) の中から選びなさい。

1. What should we have for dinner?
　(A)　I would like to go there.
　(B)　How about fish?
　(C)　She doesn't like it.

2. Did you know that Jenny will be moving to France next year?
　(A)　That's fantastic!
　(B)　France is a country in Europe.
　(C)　How often?

3. Do you know how many days are left until school starts?
　(A)　I think there are about three days left.
　(B)　He left his books on the bus.
　(C)　He is excited about starting school.

4. Is this the first volleyball game you have played?
　(A)　Why not?
　(B)　No, I have played it before.
　(C)　I think she is.

5. Why don't we get some ice cream after the movie?
　(A)　For how long?
　(B)　O.K. I'd like that.
　(C)　I had chocolate ice cream yesterday.

Part 3　Short Conversation ／会話問題

次の会話を読んで、質問に最も適当な答えを選びなさい。

質問文パターン

* Why 型パターン

1. **A**：It is almost time to go to bed. Put your pajamas on.
   B：Can we have some hot chocolate before we go to bed?
   A：No, you will not fall asleep if you have sugar before bed.

   Q：Why won't their mother let them have hot chocolate?
   a. Because she thinks it will keep them awake.
   b. Because she is not nice.
   c. Because she will give them hot chocolate.
   d. Because the children can't find their pajamas.

   解説：fall asleep「眠る」と対義語は（A）awake「目が覚める」である。

* Where 型パターン

2. **A**：Sara said to tell you hello.
   B：Oh, where did you see her?
   A：I ran into her at the jewelry store. She was buying a necklace.

   Q：Where did she see Sarah?
   a. She called her and met her at the jewelry store.
   b. She saw her by chance at the jewelry store.
   c. She bought her a necklace.
   d. She saw her at home.

   解説：run into ～「偶然出くわす」は happen to see ～と同じである。

* What 型パターン

3. **A**：I hope Veronica will be there. I want to ask her to go to the dance with me.
   B：She already has a date for the dance. She is going with Jason.
   A：Oh no! I'm too late! I should have asked her a week ago.

   Q：What does he wish he had done?
   a. Gone to the dance.
   b. Called Jason.
   c. Asked Veronica to the dance earlier.
   d. Not been late for the party.

   解説：I should have asked「誘えばよかった」と過去の行動を後悔している様子である。

* When 型パターン

4. **A**：As soon as I get paid, I am going to buy a new coat.
   B：When is your payday?
   A：The Tuesday after next.

Q：When will she buy a coat?
      a. As soon as she gets her paycheck.　　c. She's not sure.
      b. This Tuesday.　　　　　　　　　　d. Next Tuesday.

解説：get paid「給料をもらう」。Pay day「給料日」。給料は普通、銀行口座に振り込まれるか、paycheck「小切手」としてもらう。

Part 4 Short Talks／説明文問題

次の説明文の質問に最も適当な答えを選びなさい。

恥ずかしい体験

Let me tell you about an embarrassing experience I once had. When I was 12 years old, I was an actor in the school play. I practiced my part for days and days so I would remember all of the words I had to say. Finally the night of the play came. I was so excited, because my family dressed up and came to watch me. When it was my turn to speak, I was silent. I couldn't remember what to say! I took a deep breath and then ran away from the stage. I was very embarrassed.

1. Who came to watch the play?
   a. His family.   c. His teacher.
   b. His friends.   d. His boss.

2. What did he do when he forgot his words?
   a. He smiled.   c. He ran away.
   b. He dressed up. d. He went to sleep.

解説：設問1　芝居の日、話し手が興奮していた理由が because の後に述べられている。

設問2　深呼吸をした後、ran away from the stag「舞台から走り逃げた」とある。Deep breath「深呼吸」。

母親とパン

My mother is a wonderful baker. She can make bread that makes the whole house smell good. When I came home from school as a child, my mom gave me fresh, warm bread with butter. Sometimes, when it was cold outside, she made me tea to drink with my bread. Today, I am older, but every time I smell fresh bread at a bakery, I think of my mom.

1. What did her mother make for her after school?
   a. Fresh bread.   c. Cookies.
   b. Butter.   d. Pie.

2. What does she think of when she smells bread at a bakery?
   a. Her father.   c. Her mother.
   b. Tea.   d. Her childhood.

解説：設問1　彼女の母親はパンを上手に焼くことができる a wonderful baker だった。他の食べ物については話されていない。

設問2　パン屋で新鮮なパンの匂いを嗅ぐたびに I think of my mom「母親のことを考える」とある。

Part 5 Reading ／読解演習

次の段落文を読み、各設問に対して最も適切な答えを選びなさい（各段落速読問題は 2 分以内に終わらせなさい）。

スピードリーディング

In the 1960s, some young students in Amsterdam, Netherlands, thought of a good idea. They had hundreds of bicycles and gallons of white paint. They painted the bikes white, and then they placed them all around the city. They thought the local people could ride a bike wherever they needed to go. Since there were over a hundred white bikes, people could leave the bikes, and then someone else could use them.

    1. What happened after the students painted the bikes white?
        a. They rode them to school.　　　c. They sold them.
        b. They put them around the city.　d. They bought some tires.

    2. How many white bikes were there?
        a. About ten.　　　c. Over a hundred.
        b. Less than fifty.　d. Over a thousand.

In a few weeks, all of the bikes were stolen. Some people in Amsterdam developed high-tech white bikes so that they were less likely to be stolen. Each bike had a computer chip inside. In order to use the bikes, the riders needed a special card to put into the bike lock. Then, the bike lock unlocked and the rider's name was recorded in the computer chip. The security people in Amsterdam were able to know where the bike was and who was riding the bike.

    1. What happened to the white bikes?
        a. They were sold to the British.　　　　　c. They were destroyed.
        b. They were bought by a high-tech business.　d. They were stolen.

    2. What did the riders need in order to use the bikes?
        a. A license.　c. A mirror.
        b. A card.　　d. A computer chip.

The new bikes had a special appearance. They had thick pipes, bright red wheels, and very short handlebars. This appearance made it very difficult for people to steal the bikes. The bikes also had special parts, so they could not be used with other bicycles. The bike seat moved up and down, so tall and short people could ride them.

    1. What color were the wheels?
        a. White.　c. Black.
        b. Green.　d. Red.

2. Why did the bikes have special parts?

    a. So they couldn't be used with other bikes.   c. So they did not cost much to make.

    b. So they were the same color as other bikes.   d. So everyone could ride the bikes.

スピードリーディングと同じ文を読み、各設問に対して最も適切な答えを選びなさい。

読解問題

In the 1960s, some young students in Amsterdam, Netherlands, thought of a good idea. They had hundreds of bicycles and gallons of white paint. They painted the bikes white, and then they placed them all around the city. They thought the local people could ride a bike wherever they needed to go. Since there were over a hundred white bikes, people could leave the bikes, and then someone else could use them.

In a few weeks, all of the bikes were stolen. Some people in Amsterdam developed high-tech white bikes so that they were less likely to be stolen. Each bike had a computer chip inside. In order to use the bikes, the riders needed a special card to put into the bike lock. Then, the bike lock unlocked and the rider's name was recorded in the computer chip. The security people in Amsterdam were able to know where the bike was and who was riding the bike.

The new bikes had a special appearance. They had thick pipes, bright red wheels, and very short handlebars. This appearance made it very difficult for people to steal the bikes. The bikes also had special parts, so they could not be used with other bicycles. The bike seat moved up and down, so tall and short people could ride them.

After the bikes were placed in Amsterdam, people used the bikes. They saved energy and reduced traffic. Businesspeople even liked them because they got to work faster. Rather than having parents drive them, school kids rode the bikes to school with friends. The idea seemed to help the community. Unfortunately, although it was more difficult, thousands of bikes were stolen, and stealing bikes continues to be a major problem.

Comprehension Questions

1. Why did the students paint the bikes white?

    a. To help the people in the city.   c. To change the color from black.

    b. To make some money.   d. To see the bikes in the dark.

2. What was the computer chip used for?

    a. To show a map of the city and to unlock the bike.   c. To unlock the bike and record the rider's name.

    b. To find out who stole the bikes.   d. To show who needed to pay for the bike.

3. Why did the bike seats move up and down?

    a. So it was more difficult to steal.   c. So people could take them off and use a different seat.

    b. So people of different heights could ride them.   d. So people would not fall down.

4. Did the new bikes reduce the number of bikes stolen?
   a. Yes, no bikes were stolen in Amsterdam.
   b. Yes, but only for one year.
   c. No, it continues to be a big problem.
   d. No, but only ten bikes were stolen last year.

Part 6　Error Recognition／誤文訂正問題

各文には文法的誤りがあります。訂正もしくは書き換えを必要とする語句を選びなさい。

1. All of the <u>noisy</u> in the stadium made me <u>quite</u> <u>nervous</u>. There were hundreds <u>of</u> people.
　　　　　　　　A　　　　　　　　　　　　　B　　　C　　　　　　　　　　　　　　　D

   解説：前置詞（ここでは of）の後には名詞が続く。よって、下線 A には名詞 noise（雑音）が最も適切である。

   正しい英文：All of the noise in the stadium made me quite nervous. There were hundreds of people.

2. <u>May</u> you like to check your answers with <u>mine</u>? If so, we <u>can see</u> what questions gave <u>us</u> trouble.
　　 A　　　　　　　　　　　　　　　　　　　　　B　　　　　　　　　 C　　　　　　　　　　　　　　D

   解説：意味内容的に、助動詞 would が下線 A に置かれる適切な語である。Would you like to 不定詞：〜したいですか？

   正しい英文：Would you like to check your answers with mine? If so, we can see what questions gave us trouble.

3. There <u>are</u> more water on earth <u>than</u> land. In fact, <u>over</u> 70% of the earth <u>is</u> water.
　　　　　 A　　　　　　　　　　　　　 B　　　　　　　　　　C　　　　　　　　　　　　　 D

   解説：1 文目における主語 water が不可算名詞であるため、be 動詞は is であることが適切。

   正しい英文：There is more water on earth than land. In fact, over 70% of the earth is water.

4. I always go to art class <u>at</u> Mondays. I <u>feel like</u> I <u>am improving</u> my <u>drawing</u> skills.
　　　　　　　　　　　　　　 A　　　　　　　 B　　　　 C　　　　　　　　　 D

   解説：曜日（ここでは Mondays）の前に置かれる前置詞は on である。

   正しい英文：I always go to art class on Mondays. I feel like I am improving my drawing skills.

5. <u>How</u> long has it been <u>since</u> you <u>cook</u> dinner? It <u>smells</u> wonderful in here.
　　 A　　　　　　　　　　　　 B　　　　　 C　　　　　　　　　 D

   解説：How long has it been since S ＋過去形？：S が〜してどのくらいですか？

   正しい英文：How long has it been since you cooked dinner? It smells wonderful in here.

6. Lately, Ryan <u>has been</u> nightmares. He <u>had</u> one last night, and <u>he'll</u> <u>probably</u> have one tonight.
　　　　　　　　　A　　　　　　　　　　　　　 B　　　　　　　　　　　　 C　　　 D

   解説：下線 A において、現在完了進行形が不完全であるため不可である。「正しい英文」参照。

   正しい英文：Lately, Ryan has been having nightmares. He had one last night, and he'll probably have one tonight.

7. Debra enjoys <u>to be</u> outside <u>in</u> the sun, and Jackie <u>does</u>, <u>too</u>.
　　　　　　　　　 A　　　　　　　 B　　　　　　　　　　　　 C　　 D

   解説：enjoy -ing：〜することを楽しむ。

   正しい英文：Debra enjoys being outside in the sun, and Jackie does, too.

Part 7　Incomplete Sentence／文法・語彙問題

文法的に適切な語句を1つ選び、文を完成させなさい。

1. Tomorrow I _____ to class. The teacher is giving a test.
    a. am having to go　　c. have to go
    b. can go　　　　　　d. may go

   訳：明日授業へ行かなければならない。先生はテストを与える。
   解説：意味内容的に、c. have to go が空欄に入る最も適切な語。have（has）to do：〜しなければならない（通例進行形にはしない）

2. I _____ a lot when I'm nervous.
    a. usually am talking　　c. talking
    b. talk usual　　　　　　d. usually talk

   訳：私は緊張しているときたくさん話す。
   解説：文法的に、d. usually talk が空欄に入る最も適切な語である。副詞（ここでは usually）は通例動詞の直前に置かれる。

3. I hope that _____ to Stanford University. I should find out soon.
    a. I am being accepted　　c. I accepted
    b. I will be accepted　　　d. I had been accepted

   訳：スタンフォード大学に合格することを望んでいる。もうすぐ分かるはずだ。
   解説：意味内容的に、b. I will be accepted が空欄に入る最も適切な語である。また、空欄には、意味内容から、「未来」の事柄が述べられなければ意味が通らないことにも注意しよう。be accepted to：（学校など）に合格する

4. My nephew is _____ child.
    a. rather spoiled　　c. a rather
    b. spoiled rather　　d. a rather spoiled

   訳：私の甥は結構甘やかされている子供だ。
   解説：ここで用いられている rather（結構）は副詞であるため、意味内容から spoiled を修飾していると考えられるので、d. a rather spoiled が空欄に入る最も適切な語である。

5. The employees complained about _____ enough time to complete the projects.
    a. ever having　　c. never having
    b. to have　　　　d. ever have

   訳：従業員たちは、その企画を完成させる十分な時間が無いことに不平を言った。
   解説：前置詞（ここでは about）の後には名詞（動名詞も含む）が置かれる。よって、動名詞 c. never having が空欄に入る最も適切な語である。

Lesson 8 (http://audio.lincenglish.com にアクセスして音声を聞いてください)

Part 1　Image Listening／写真描写問題

1. 左の写真を見て、人物の行動や物の位置などについて文を3つ作りなさい。
　_____
　_____
　_____

2. 写真の描写文として最も適切な文をA～Dの中から選びなさい。
　(A)，(B)，(C)，(D)

1. 左の写真を見て、人物の行動や物の位置などについて文を3つ作りなさい。
　_____
　_____
　_____

2. 写真の描写文として最も適切な文をA～Dの中から選びなさい。
　(A)，(B)，(C)，(D)

1. 左の写真を見て、人物の行動や物の位置などについて文を3つ作りなさい。
　_____
　_____
　_____

2. 写真の描写文として最も適切な文をA～Dの中から選びなさい。
　(A)，(B)，(C)，(D)

1. 左の写真を見て、人物の行動や物の位置などについて文を3つ作りなさい。
　_____
　_____
　_____

2. 写真の描写文として最も適切な文をA～Dの中から選びなさい。
　(A)，(B)，(C)，(D)

Part 2 Question and Response ／質疑応答問題

重要な質問表現

How long have you been a teacher?
　　職務勤続年数をきかれている。

Have you ever been to China?
　　中国への旅行経験の有無をきいている質問。

How many cats do you have?
　　飼っている猫の数を答える。

What time do you go to bed?
　　就寝時間をきかれている。

What did you think of the movie last night?
　　"what do/did you think of 〜 ?" は映画の感想を尋ねるのによく使われる表現。

How often do you wash your car?
　　車を洗う頻度を答える。

What are you eating?
　　「食べているもの」は何かを答える。

Have you ever tried shrimp?
　　エビを食べたことがあるかの経験をきかれている。

What kind of ice cream do you like?
　　好きなアイスクリームの種類を答える。

Why don't we go for a walk?
　　go for a walk「散歩に行く」。または take a walk ともいう。

確認ドリル

次の1〜5の質問に対して最も適切な応答をそれぞれ (A)〜(C) の中から選びなさい。

1. Can you play the guitar?
   (A) I am a good singer.
   (B) No, I can't.
   (C) He is in the band.

2. When do you want to go to the movie?
   (A) Someday I will see it.
   (B) Follow me.
   (C) Saturday is best.

3. Who came to your house last night?
   (A) She is always late.
   (B) She will be here tomorrow.
   (C) My sister came over.

4. Are you wearing my earrings?
   (A) Yes, I borrowed them from your room.
   (B) I don't like it.
   (C) This is my pen.

5. Could you please turn the radio up?
   (A) I love to sing.
   (B) It is loud enough already.
   (C) Who sings this song?

Part 3 Short Conversation／会話問題

次の会話を読んで、質問に最も適当な答えを選びなさい。

質問文パターン

* What 型パターン

1. **A**：Maria, there is a woman here to see you about the car.
   B：Thank you, Steven. I hope she wants to buy it.
   A：She looks like she is very interested in buying it.

   Q：What is Maria selling?
   　　a. Apples.　　c. A car.
   　　b. Boats.　　d. A house.

   解説：〈be interested in 動詞＋ing〉の形をおさらいしよう。

* Why 型パターン

2. **A**：Do you want to go to the gym with me?
   B：I prefer to go jogging outside. I like the fresh air.
   A：O.K. Let's go jog outside together then.

   Q：Why does he like to go jogging outside instead of to the gym?
   　　a. Because it's free.　　c. Because he prefers the gym.
   　　b. Because he likes the fresh air.　　d. Because the gym is too busy.

   解説：prefer to ～「～（の方を）好む」。

* Who 型パターン

3. **A**：Do you know why I stopped you?
   B：No, officer. Was I driving too fast?
   A：Yes. You were driving 80 kilometers per hour. The speed limit is 60 kilometers per hour.

   Q：Who are the people talking?
   　　a. A father and a daughter.　　c. A police officer and a driver.
   　　b. A teacher and a student.　　d. Two friends.

   解説：スピード違反で捕まっている様子。

* When 型パターン

4. **A**：Mr. Roberts, I am finished with my report. Is there anything else I can do?
   B：No, you have done enough. Thank you for your hard work, Mrs. Peterson.
   A：No problem. I will see you next week.

Q：When will they see each other again?
- a. Next week.
- c. In a month.
- b. Tomorrow.
- d. In an hour.

解説：会話最後に注目しよう。See you next week「また来週」。

Part 4　Short Talks ／説明文問題

次の説明文の質問に最も適当な答えを選びなさい。

フランスのチーズ

France is famous for making cheese. There are more than 360 different kinds of cheese made in France. Some are sweet, and some have a very strong flavor. Some cheeses are soft, while others are hard. French cheese is made from the milk of cows, sheep or goats. French people like to eat cheese with bread, often as dessert with fruit. One of the most famous cheeses in France is called Roquefort, which is made in the south of France.

1. How many kinds of cheese are made in France?
   a. Less than thirty.　　　　c. More than four hundred.
   b. More than three hundred.　d. Over one thousand.

2. Where is Roquefort made?
   a. In the west of France.　　c. In the east of France.
   b. In the south of France.　　d. In the north of France.

解説：設問1　本文で数字がたくさん出てくるというわけではないので問題ないだろう。Less than ～「～以下」、more than ～「～以上」という言い方を確認しておこう。

設問2　the south of France は southern France と同意語である。両方の言い方を使えるようにしておこう。

ビック・スカイカントリー "モンタナ"

Montana is a beautiful place. There are mountains and rivers and lakes nearby, and people are very friendly. People from all around the world come to see the nature and to go skiing and visit Yellowstone National Park. In the summer, people go fishing, hiking, camping and boating, and in the winter, many people go skiing. There is not much crime, and the air is very clean. Montana's nickname is "The Big Sky Country."

1. What do people do in the winter?
   a. Go fishing.　　c. Go camping.
   b. Go skiing.　　d. Go boating.

2. What is Montana's nickname?
   a. The Big Sky Country.　　c. Yellowstone National Park.
   b. Happy Land.　　　　　　d. A Friendly Place.

解説：設問1　選択肢の中で冬にできることといえばスキーのみである。

設問2　County は「郡」という意味である。ルイジアナ州とアラスカ州を除く各州の最大行政区画を指す。ルイジアナ州では parish、アラスカ州では borough がこれに相当する。米国留学を控えている際など、自分の留学先の州での区画単語が何か覚えておくと便利。

Part 5　Reading ／読解演習

次の段落文を読み、各設問に対して最も適切な答えを選びなさい（各段落速読問題は 2 分以内に終わらせなさい）。

スピードリーディング

　The Great Lakes are five very big lakes in eastern North America. They are, in fact, the biggest group of fresh water lakes in the world. This means that the water is not salty, unlike the water of the ocean. The Great Lakes are Lake Huron, Lake Michigan, Lake Superior, Lake Erie, and Lake Ontario. They are sometimes called the inland seas.

　　1. Where are the Great Lakes located?
　　　　a. In western Canada.　　　c. In eastern North America.
　　　　b. In Michigan.　　　　　　d. In western North America.

　　2. What is a fresh water lake?
　　　　a. A lake that does not have a lot of salt.　　c. A lake that helps the farmers grow fruit.
　　　　b. A new lake for people to go swimming.　　d. A lake that is next to the ocean.

　Four of the Great Lakes are shared between Canada and the United States of America. Lake Michigan is the only one that is all inside the United States. Water from Lake Superior and Lake Michigan flows into Lake Huron. The water eventually goes to the Atlantic Ocean.

　　1. Who shares the Great Lakes?
　　　　a. Michigan and Huron.　　　c. Canada and the U.S.
　　　　b. Canada and Mexico.　　　　d. Michigan and Superior.

　　2. Where does the water from Lake Superior and Lake Michigan flow?
　　　　a. To Canada.　　　　　　　c. Into Lake Union.
　　　　b. Into the Pacific Ocean.　　d. Into Lake Huron.

　There are the approximately 35,000 islands within the Great Lakes. Manitoulin Island, which is located in Lake Huron, is the largest island in the Great Lakes. Today, 20 percent of the world's fresh water is in the five Great Lakes. The lakes change the weather in the area. In the winter, the snow can be very heavy because there is a lot of moisture in the air. In the summer, the air can be a little cooler in the U.S. states that are near the Great Lakes.

　　1. How many islands are in the Great Lakes?
　　　　a. 3,500.　　　c. 35,000.
　　　　b. 350.　　　　d. 3.5 million

　　2. What in the area is changed by the lakes?
　　　　a. The shape.　　　c. The attitude.
　　　　b. The weather.　　d. The smell of the air.

スピードリーディングと同じ文を読み、各設問に対して最も適切な答えを選びなさい。

読解問題

The Great Lakes are five very big lakes in eastern North America. They are, in fact, the biggest group of fresh water lakes in the world. This means that the water is not salty, unlike the water of the ocean. The Great Lakes are Lake Huron, Lake Michigan, Lake Superior, Lake Erie, and Lake Ontario. They are sometimes called the inland seas.

Four of the Great Lakes are shared between Canada and the United States of America. Lake Michigan is the only one that is all inside the United States. Water from Lake Superior and Lake Michigan flows into Lake Huron. The water eventually goes to the Atlantic Ocean.

There are the approximately 35,000 islands within the Great Lakes. Manitoulin Island, which is located in Lake Huron, is the largest island in the Great Lakes. Today, 20 percent of the world's fresh water is in the five Great Lakes. The lakes change the weather in the area. In the winter, the snow can be very heavy because there is a lot of moisture in the air. In the summer, the air can be a little cooler in the U.S. states that are near the Great Lakes.

The Great Lakes are used mainly for transportation. Many businesses have large boats, called cargo ships, to transport products to other states. However, the number of cargo ships on the Great Lakes is decreasing. The reason there are fewer cargo ships is because many businesses use land transportation, such as trains and trucks, to transport products. Many people also use the Great Lakes for fun. Sailing and fishing are quite popular activities in the area.

Comprehension Questions

1. What are the Great Lakes sometimes called?
   a. The big lakes.   c. The fresh waters.
   b. The inland seas.   d. The inland shores.

2. Where does the water from the Great Lakes flow?
   a. Into the Atlantic Ocean.   c. Into Canada.
   b. Into the Pacific Ocean.   d. Into the eastern part of Michigan.

3. Why is the snow heavy in the wintertime?
   a. Because the lakes are near Canada.   c. Because of the dark clouds.
   b. Because there is not a lot of sunlight. d. Because of the moisture in the air.

4. Why is the number of cargo ships decreasing?
   a. Businesses do not want to buy gas.   c. Businesses use land transportation more.
   b. Businesses are not safe on the boats.   d. Businesses do not ship to Canada.

Part 6　Error Recognition ／誤文訂正問題

各文には文法的誤りがあります。訂正もしくは書き換えを必要とする語句を選びなさい。

1. Tony sometimes <u>walk</u> to school. When his father <u>doesn't</u> have to work, <u>then</u> he <u>drives</u>.
　　　　　　　　　　A　　　　　　　　　　　　　　　　B　　　　　　　　　　　C　　　　D

　　解説：1 文目における主語 Tony が三人称であることから、あとに続く動詞には三単元 -s が必要である。よって、walk<u>s</u> が下線 A に置かれる適切な語となる。

　　正しい英文：Tony sometimes walks to school. When his father doesn't have to work, then he drives.

2. I <u>leaved</u> work <u>around</u> 5:30. After that, I <u>took</u> the bus to the gym and <u>worked out</u> for an hour.
　　　A　　　　　B　　　　　　　　　　　　　　C　　　　　　　　　　　　　　　D

　　解説：to leave（去る）：leave（現在）-left（過去）-left（過去分詞）。

　　正しい英文：I left work around 5:30. After that, I took the bus to the gym and worked out for an hour.

3. Last year, we all <u>went</u> to <u>the</u> Pacific Ocean <u>for</u> two weeks. Everyone in my family <u>like</u> to swim.
　　　　　　　　　　A　　　B　　　　　　　　　　C　　　　　　　　　　　　　　　　　　D

　　解説：everyone は単数扱い。よって、その動詞 like には三単元 -s が必要となる。

　　正しい英文：Last year, we all went to the Pacific Ocean for two weeks. Everyone in my family likes to swim.

4. I haven't <u>never</u> been <u>to</u> Arizona, but I plan <u>to travel</u> <u>there</u> next year.
　　　　　　　A　　　　　B　　　　　　　　　　　C　　　　D

　　解説：not ever（決して〜ない）で「完全否定」を意味する（=never）。

　　正しい英文：I haven't ever been to Arizona, but I plan to travel there next year.

5. I <u>can</u> speak Arabic, and so can <u>her</u>. We <u>have been taking</u> classes <u>for</u> two years.
　　　A　　　　　　　　　　　　　　B　　　　　　C　　　　　　　　　　　D

　　解説：下線 B における語は主格であるため、she が適切である。問 13 参照。

　　正しい英文：I can speak Arabic, and so can she.　We have been taking classes for two years.

6. That coffee is <u>too hotter</u>. I <u>will wait</u> a few minutes <u>so that</u> it <u>cools off</u>.
　　　　　　　　　　A　　　　　　B　　　　　　　　　　　C　　　　　D

　　解説：副詞 too は比較級（ここでは faster）を修飾することはできない。

　　正しい英文：That coffee is too hot. I will wait a few minutes so that it cools off.

7. <u>It</u> is an <u>embarrassing</u> story, so I'd rather not <u>mentioned</u> why I was <u>late</u>.
　　A　　　　　B　　　　　　　　　　　　　　　　C　　　　　　　　　　D

　　解説：I would/had rather 原形：（どちらかというと）〜したい。

　　正しい英文：It is an embarrassing story, so I'd rather not mention why I was late.

Part 7　Incomplete Sentence／文法・語彙問題

文法的に適切な語句を1つ選び、文を完成させなさい。

1. That bowl _____ wood.
    - a. is made of
    - b. makes with
    - c. is making of
    - d. makes out of

訳：そのボウルは木でできている。
解説：be made of 〜：〜でできている。

2. My car is in the shop. _____, I'll take the bus to work.
    - a. Mainly
    - b. In order to
    - c. In the meantime
    - d. As a matter of fact

訳：私の車は修理所にあります。その間、職場まではバスを使う。
解説：文脈から、c. In the meantime（その間）が空欄に入る最も適切な語。訳参照。

3. If you head to the store, could you pick up a _____ of cereal?
    - a. container
    - b. gallon
    - c. box
    - d. bowl

訳：もしその店に行くなら、シリアルを1箱買ってきてくれませんか？
解説：cereal（シリアル）はbox（箱）に入っていることから、c. boxが空欄に入る最も適切な語である。

4. Charles doesn't like horror films, and Connie _____.
    - a. don't either
    - b. doesn't either
    - c. don't also
    - d. doesn't neither

訳：チャールズはホラー映画が好きではないし、コニーもだ。
解説：not, eitherは否定に対する同意として用いられる表現である。また、主語Connieが三人称であることから、動詞には三単元-sが必要であることにも注意しよう。それらを考慮に入れると、b. doesn't eitherが空欄に入る最も適切な語と推測できる。

5. We ordered too much food last night, so now we have _____ for tomorrow.
    - a. food extra
    - b. servings
    - c. cartons
    - d. leftovers

訳：昨晩食べ物を注文しすぎたので、明日のための残り物がある。
解説：文脈から、名詞d. leftovers（料理の残り物）が空欄に入る最も適切な語である。訳参照。

Lesson 9 (http://audio.lincenglish.com にアクセスして音声を聞いてください)

Part 1　Image Listening／写真描写問題

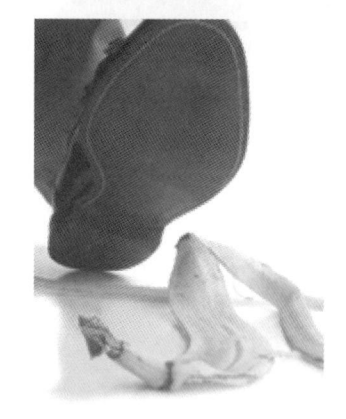

1. 左の写真を見て、人物の行動や物の位置などについて文を3つ作りなさい。

2. 写真の描写文として最も適切な文をA〜Dの中から選びなさい。
　(A), (B), (C), (D)

1. 左の写真を見て、人物の行動や物の位置などについて文を3つ作りなさい。

2. 写真の描写文として最も適切な文をA〜Dの中から選びなさい。
　(A), (B), (C), (D)

1. 左の写真を見て、人物の行動や物の位置などについて文を3つ作りなさい。

2. 写真の描写文として最も適切な文をA〜Dの中から選びなさい。
　(A), (B), (C), (D)

1. 左の写真を見て、人物の行動や物の位置などについて文を3つ作りなさい。

2. 写真の描写文として最も適切な文をA〜Dの中から選びなさい。
　(A), (B), (C), (D)

Part 2 Question and Response／質疑応答問題

重要な質問表現

How many times have you seen this movie?
映画を見た回数をきかれている。

How about some coffee?
もう1杯のコーヒーを勧められている場面である。

Who lives next door?
next door「隣人、ご近所さん」。

Who taught you how to play piano?
「弾き方を教えた」人物に関して答える。

Who has their books with them?
「誰が」「本を」持っているか。

Can you meet me at 7:00?
「会える」可能性をきいている。

Did you take a bath last night?
take a bath/showers「お風呂に入る、シャワーを浴びる」。

Do you think I made a mistake?
make a mistake「間違える」。

Would you like me to call you later?
would you like 人 to ～「(人)に～してほしい」。

How old is your son?
単純に「息子」の「年齢」を答える。

確認ドリル

次の1～5の質問に対して最も適切な応答をそれぞれ (A)～(C) の中から選びなさい。

1. How is your father doing?
   (A) His name is Scot.
   (B) He is an artist.
   (C) He is doing well.

2. Who owns these books?
   (A) They are romantic books.
   (B) The books are funny.
   (C) The books belong to Sharron.

3. Which one is your brother?
   (A) The guy with the blue shirt on.
   (B) I am younger than my brother.
   (C) I am his sister.

4. When did you start to learn English?
   (A) When I was a child.
   (B) I am learning French.
   (C) English is fun to learn.

5. Did you have a good day at school?
   (A) It was OK.
   (B) I wonder why.
   (C) I walked to school.

Part 3　Short Conversation ／会話問題

次の会話を読んで、質問に最も適当な答えを選びなさい。

質問文パターン

* Where 型パターン

1. **A**：Here is the furniture that you ordered. Where would you like me to put the sofa?
   B：Please put it in the living room, by the window.
   A：O.K. I will put the table and chairs in the kitchen for now.

   Q：Where will he put the table and chairs?
   　　　a. In the bedroom.　　c. In the living room.
   　　　b. In the kitchen.　　d. In the family room.

   解説：ソファーは居間に、テーブルとイスは台所に置いている。For now「今のところ」。

* Why 型パターン

2. **A**：The music here is too loud. It is hurting my ears!
   B：Do you want to leave the club? We can go somewhere a little quieter. Max's Club is quiet but not boring.
   A：That would be great. I can't hear you talk.

   Q：Why are they leaving?
   　　　a. Because the club is dirty.　　c. Because the club is boring.
   　　　b. Because the club is fun.　　　d. Because the club is too loud.

   解説：hear は使役動詞としても使われ、〈hear　人　動詞原形〉で「人が～（動詞）するのが聞こえる」となる。

* When 型パターン

3. **A**：Excuse me, ma'am. When does the bus to the mall arrive?
   B：It comes every thirty minutes. The last one was here twenty minutes ago.
   A：Good. I only need to wait ten more minutes.

   Q：When does the next bus come?
   　　　a. In thirty minutes.　　c. In twenty minutes.
   　　　b. In ten minutes.　　　d. In twenty-five minutes.

   解説：会話文頭の ma'am は通常「お嬢さん、奥様、お客様」など丁寧な呼びかけとして用いられる。

* What 型パターン

4. **A**：This room is very messy! You need to clean it up. There is garbage everywhere!

   B：I will, but first I want to watch my movie.

   A：You can watch the movie after you take the garbage out. You can clean the rest of your room this evening after the movie.

   Q：What must he do before he watches the movie?
   - a. Watch a movie.
   - b. Clean his entire room
   - c. Read a book.
   - d. Take out the garbage in his room.

解説：take out「〜を取り去る」。

Part 4　Short Talks／説明文問題

次の説明文の質問に最も適当な答えを選びなさい。

ケチャップ

Ketchup is a sauce made from tomatoes that is very popular in the United States and in other countries. The basic ingredients are tomatoes, vinegar, sugar and salt. American people like to put ketchup on hamburgers, French fries and hot dogs. It is both sweet and salty, and many people like it with mustard. I always keep a bottle of ketchup at my house!

1. What is the most important ingredient in ketchup?
   a. Salt.　　　　c. Sugar.
   b. Tomatoes.　　d. Vinegar.

2. How does ketchup taste?
   a. Sour.　　　　　c. Bitter.
   b. Sweet and salty.　d. Delicious.

解説：設問1　すべての選択肢は The basic ingredients として紹介されたが、その前の文で made from tomatoes「トマトから作られている」とあるように、トマトが主原料である。
　　　設問2　ケチャップの味は both sweet and salty と表現する。他の選択肢の英語での言い方も覚えておこう。

いろいろな食べ方

In different countries, people have different ways of eating food. In some countries, people use two sticks called "chopsticks" to eat things like noodles. Many people in Asia use chopsticks made of wood, plastic or metal. In other countries, such as Europe and the United States, people use a fork and a knife to eat. In countries such as Saudi Arabia, people eat without a tool. Instead, they use their right hand to eat the food. It is fun to try to eat in a different way!

1. What are the two sticks called?
   a. Forks.　　　c. Noodles.
   b. Chopsticks.　d. Knives.

2. How do people in Saudi Arabia sometimes eat food?
   a. With chopsticks.　　c. With the right hand.
   b. With a cup.　　　　d. With a napkin.

解説：設問1　日本人が毎日使う箸は、2本で1膳のセットなので常に複数形にするべきである。Knives の単数形は knife。バターなどを塗るナイフは butter knife「バターナイフ」と呼ばれる。
　　　設問2　サウジアラビアの人びとは without a tool「道具なし」で食事をするという。

Part 5　Reading／読解演習

次の段落文を読み、各設問に対して最も適切な答えを選びなさい（各段落速読問題は 2 分以内に終わらせなさい）。

スピードリーディング

　Many people prefer to eat food from their own culture because they are familiar with it. Some people dislike certain foods because they are not accustomed to it. For example, Australians like the taste of grilled crocodile. The people from Australia use the meat from a crocodile's tail and then cook the meat. Pizza is one of the most common types of food in America, but many Asians strongly dislike this popular American food. Many Saudi Arabian people eat camel on special occasions. However, this animal is not commonly found in the U.S. or several other countries.

1. Why might a man dislike a certain food?
   a. Because he is not accustomed to it.
   b. Because he is familiar with it.
   c. Because it's from his culture.
   d. Because it's cooked wrong.

2. What part of the crocodile do the Australians cook?
   a. The legs.
   b. The body.
   c. The tail.
   d. The arms.

　People may only eat certain foods for religious reasons. For Hindus, the cow is a sacred animal, so they do not eat beef. Muslims and Jewish people do not eat pork or any pork products because they believe pigs are unclean animals. Furthermore, people may not eat at all for a short period of time because of religious beliefs. This is called *fasting*. In the Catholic religion, some believers fast on certain holy days as a sign of sacrifice. Religion is connected to culture, and it sometimes explains why people eat only certain foods at certain times.

1. Why don't Hindus eat beef?
   a. Because they are vegetarians.
   b. Because they don't eat any meat.
   c. Because they believe the cow is sacred.
   d. Because they think it is not necessary.

2. What is it called when a person doesn't eat for a little while?
   a. Binging.
   b. Fasting.
   c. Praying.
   d. Worshipping.

　Research has suggested that people prefer the food that they grew up with. What is available in the area also affects a person's daily diet. Typically, if a person lives close to the ocean, then seafood is a staple in the diet. If a person lives inland, animal meat and vegetables raised on a farm are commonly part of the main diet. Food that may be strange to one culture may be very normal to another culture. For example, in Africa, some people eat insects and termites, while in Asia, some people eat dog meat. The type of food that people eat is different in every country.

1. According to research, what do people prefer?
    a. Food from childhood.
    b. Food from other cultures.
    c. New and strange foods.
    d. A variety of food from other countries.

2. What interesting food do some Asians eat?
    a. Pizza.
    b. Termites.
    c. Insects.
    d. Dog meat.

スピードリーディングと同じ文を読み、各設問に対して最も適切な答えを選びなさい。

読解問題

Many people prefer to eat food from their own culture because they are familiar with it. Some people dislike certain foods because they are not accustomed to it. For example, Australians like the taste of grilled crocodile. The people from Australia use the meat from a crocodile's tail and then cook the meat. Pizza is one of the most common types of food in America, but many Asians strongly dislike this popular American food. Many Saudi Arabian people eat camel on special occasions. However, this animal is not commonly found in the U.S. or several other countries.

People may only eat certain foods for religious reasons. For Hindus, the cow is a sacred animal, so they do not eat beef. Muslims and Jewish people do not eat pork or any pork products because they believe pigs are unclean animals. Furthermore, people may not eat at all for a short period of time because of religious beliefs. This is called *fasting*. In the Catholic religion, some believers fast on certain holy days as a sign of sacrifice. Religion is connected to culture, and it sometimes explains why people eat only certain foods at certain times.

Research has suggested that people prefer the food that they grew up with. What is available in the area also affects a person's daily diet. Typically, if a person lives close to the ocean, then seafood is a staple in the diet. If a person lives inland, animal meat and vegetables raised on a farm are commonly part of the main diet. Food that may be strange to one culture may be very normal to another culture. For example, in Africa, some people eat insects and termites, while in Asia, some people eat dog meat. The type of food that people eat is different in every country.

Sometimes people need to adapt to new eating habits. If we live in a different culture for an extended period of time, we may have to eat what is available in the area. As a result, the food in the new culture may be very different than the food we grew up with as a child. As time passes, we get used to the strange food because it becomes familiar. However, many people still dream about mom's home cooking and the local food when they leave their home environment.

Comprehension Questions

1. What is a food that a Chinese person probably wouldn't like, but an American would love?
    a. Chicken.
    b. Pizza.
    c. Hamburgers.
    d. Dog meat.

2. What animal is considered dirty in the Jewish religion?

    a. Cow.   c. Pig.

    b. Dog.   d. Ram.

3. Why do people from Africa eat insects and termites?

    a. Because they like to try new food.   c. Because they are healthy.

    b. Because it is normal to them.   d. Because they live by a large body of water.

4. The word "extended" in the second sentence of the fourth paragraph is closest in meaning to what word?

    a. Short.   c. Strange.

    b. Different.   d. Long.

Part 6　Error Recognition／誤文訂正問題

各文には文法的誤りがあります。訂正もしくは書き換えを必要とする語句を選びなさい。

1. In a <u>many</u> days, <u>I'll</u> be 15 years old! I will <u>finally</u> <u>be able</u> to drive!
　　　　　A　　　　　B　　　　　　　　　　　　　　　C　　　D

　　解説：意味内容から、few が空欄に入る最も適切な語である。a few：少しの　in a few days：数日以内で
　　正しい英文：In a few days, I'll be 15 years old! I will finally be able to drive!

2. Last night, I <u>cooked</u> dinner <u>when</u> I got home. Then, I <u>made</u> a shower <u>after that</u>.
　　　　　　　　　A　　　　　　　B　　　　　　　　　　　　　　C　　　　　　　D

　　解説：take a shower：シャワーを浴びる
　　正しい英文：Last night, I cooked dinner when I got home. Then, I took a shower after that.

3. Who <u>has studied</u> English <u>the longest</u>—Roberto or Yukari? Both of them <u>are</u> <u>excellent</u> students.
　　　　　　A　　　　　　　　　　B　　　　　　　　　　　　　　　　　　　　　C　　　D

　　解説：意味内容的に、下線 B には比較級 longer が適切な語である。訳参照。
　　正しい英文：Who has studied English longer—Roberto or Yukari? Both of them are excellent students.

4. I <u>know</u> you go to school, but what <u>else</u> have you <u>doing</u> <u>lately</u>?
　　　A　　　　　　　　　　　　　　　B　　　　　　　C　　　D

　　解説：but 以下の節が不完全な現在完了進行形（have（has）been＋-ing）となっているため、下線 C が誤りである。
　　正しい英文：I know you go to school, but what else have you been doing lately?

5. Where <u>have you been</u>? I <u>have waiting</u> for you for two hours! You <u>should</u> have called <u>me</u>.
　　　　　　　A　　　　　　　　　　B　　　　　　　　　　　　　　　　　　C　　　　　　　　D

　　解説：下線 B において、現在完了進行形が不完全であることに注意しよう。正しい英文参照。
　　正しい英文：Where have you been? I have been waiting for you for two hours! You should have called me.

6. This year <u>Becky's</u> garden is <u>full of</u> carrots, beans, and corn. Becky <u>didn't grew</u> any <u>vegetables</u> last year.
　　　　　　　　A　　　　　　　　B　　　　　　　　　　　　　　　　　　　　　　C　　　　　　　D

　　解説：下線 C において、助動詞 did があるため動詞は原形 grow であることが適切である。
　　正しい英文：This year Becky's garden is full of carrots, beans, and corn. Becky didn't grow any vegetables last year.

7. I <u>get usually up</u> at 7:00. However, on the <u>weekends</u> I <u>sleep in</u> <u>until</u> 11:00.
　　　　　　A　　　　　　　　　　　　　　　　　　B　　　　C　　　　D

　　解説：通例、副詞（ここでは usually）は動詞（get up（起床する））の直前に置かれる。
　　正しい英文：I usually get up at 7:00. However, on the weekends I sleep in until 11:00.

Part 7　Incomplete Sentence／文法・語彙問題

文法的に適切な語句を1つ選び、文を完成させなさい。

1. If you don't want the ice cream to melt, you should keep it _____.
    - a. freezer
    - b. freezing
    - c. frozen
    - d. freezes

訳：アイスクリームが溶けてほしくないなら、それを冷凍しておくべきです。
解説：keep O 過去分詞：O が〜されたままにしておく freeze（現在）- froze（過去）- frozen（過去分詞）

2. His story doesn't make any _____. He said he was sick, but I saw him at the party.
    - a. solution
    - b. information
    - c. sense
    - d. idea

訳：彼の話は意味が分からない。彼は病気だったと言ったが、パーティーで彼を見た。
解説：「make sense：意味を成す」はよく用いられる表現なので覚えておくと便利である。

3. Some people have a _____ when they try to stop smoking.
    - a. hard time
    - b. powerful time
    - c. smooth time
    - d. big time

訳：禁煙しようとするとき、苦労する人もいる。
解説：意味内容から、a. hard time が空欄に入る最も適切な語である。have a hard time：苦労する

4. It is almost _____ to imagine life without computers because we rely on them so much.
    - a. unbelievable
    - b. contrary
    - c. impossible
    - d. difficulty

訳：私たちはパソコンに非常に頼っているので、パソコンの無い人生を想像するなんてあり得ない。
解説：ここでは形式主語 it が用いられていることに注意しよう。it は to 不定詞以下（to imagine life...）の内容を指す。よって、文脈から、形容詞 c. impossible（不可能な）が空欄に入る最も適切な語である。（注釈：形式主語 it が用いられる例：It is very important to learn a foreign language at an early age.／早くに外国語を学ぶ事は非常に重要だ。主語 it は to 不定詞以下の内容を指す。「それ」とは訳さない。）

5. Have you seen my sunglasses? I can't find them _____.
    - a. somewhere
    - b. anywhere
    - c. nowhere
    - d. everywhere

訳：私のサングラスを見た？　どこにも見つからないの。
解説：not と any は完全否定を表すために呼応して用いられる。I do not have any money with me right now.／今お金がまったくない。

88

Lesson 10 (http://audio.lincenglish.com にアクセスして音声を聞いてください)

Part 1　Image Listening／写真描写問題

1. 左の写真を見て、人物の行動や物の位置などについて文を3つ作りなさい。
   _____
   _____
   _____

2. 写真の描写文として最も適切な文をA～Dの中から選びなさい。
   (A)，(B)，(C)，(D)

1. 左の写真を見て、人物の行動や物の位置などについて文を3つ作りなさい。
   _____
   _____
   _____

2. 写真の描写文として最も適切な文をA～Dの中から選びなさい。
   (A)，(B)，(C)，(D)

1. 左の写真を見て、人物の行動や物の位置などについて文を3つ作りなさい。
   _____
   _____
   _____

2. 写真の描写文として最も適切な文をA～Dの中から選びなさい。
   (A)，(B)，(C)，(D)

1. 左の写真を見て、人物の行動や物の位置などについて文を3つ作りなさい。
   _____
   _____
   _____

2. 写真の描写文として最も適切な文をA～Dの中から選びなさい。
   (A)，(B)，(C)，(D)

Part 2 Question and Response／質疑応答問題

重要な質問表現

Are there any parks by your house?
　　by ～「～のそばに」なので by your house で「あなたの家のそばに」となる。

Have you ever tried Mexican food?
　　yes/noで答えられる質問では、yes/noを使おう。使わないとしても Of course!「もちろん！」などで yes/no どちらかなのかはっきりと意思表示をするようにしよう。

When do we get our paychecks?
　　paycheck「給料小切手、給料」。Salary も「報酬、給料」という意味だが、アメリカでは小切手が頻繁に使われ、給料も小切手で支払われることが多い。その際は get my paycheck で給料が支払われるということを表せる。

Do you enjoy nature?
　　何か物事が好きかどうか聞く際に、like「好き」という単語の代わりに enjoy「楽しむ」という単語を使うことも可能である。

How did you lose weight?
　　lose weight「体重が減る」の反対の意味は gain weight「体重が増える」である。

Do you want to see my house?
　　「～しませんか？」と人を誘うときは、do you want to ～ と遠まわしに提案することがある。

Would you like me to take you home?
　　take one home「〈人〉を家に送る」。

How many children does she have?
　　何人の子どもがいるか聞かれている。

When is it going to rain?
　　今後雨が降るのはいつになるかの会話である。

Who is that man?
　　男性がどういう人で何をしているかではなく、誰かということを聞いている。

確認ドリル

次の１～５の質問に対して最も適切な応答をそれぞれ（A）～（C）の中から選びなさい。

1. Would you like to have an expensive car?
   (A) Oh, wow!
   (B) Today he will give me a ride.
   (C) Of course I would.

2. Who cut the grass?
   (A) He is at home.
   (B) The boy next door.
   (C) That's enough.

3. Did you remember to buy some sugar?
   (A) I am going to make dessert.
   (B) I completely forgot.
   (C) I love sweets.

4. Why weren't you on time?
   (A) I am here for the meeting.
   (B) She is at work.
   (C) I slept too late.

5. Are you kidding?
   (A) I don't have any.
   (B) No, I am serious.
   (C) Why not?

Part 3　Short Conversation／会話問題

次の会話を読んで、質問に最も適当な答えを選びなさい。

質問文パターン

＊ When 型パターン

1. **A**：Can I borrow your black dress for the party tonight?
   B：Sure. It is in my closet.
   A：I will return it tomorrow.

   Q：When will she return the dress?
   　　a. Tonight.　　c. Next week.
   　　b. Tomorrow.　　d. Yesterday.

解説：今夜のパーティーのためにドレスを借り、明日返すつもりのようだ。

＊ Who 型パターン

2. **A**：Hi, Susan. I'm Jonathon. I am Brian's brother.
   B：Nice to meet you.
   A：Nice to meet you, too.

   Q：Who is Jonathon's brother?
   　　a. Susan.　　c. Brian.
   　　b. Jonathon.　　d. Jeff.

解説：選択肢でたくさんの名前が出てくるので混乱しないようにしよう。

＊ Why 型パターン

3. **A**：What kind of movie do you want to watch, an action or a comedy?
   B：I'd like to see a comedy. I want to laugh.
   A：O.K. I feel like laughing tonight, too.

   Q：Why do they agree on a comedy?
   　　a. Because they want to laugh.　　c. Because they don't like action movies.
   　　b. Because they want to cry.　　d. Because the movie starts too late.

解説：feel like 〜 ing「〜したい気分」。どういった映画を観るか決めようとしている。

＊ Where 型パターン

4. **A**：I have two tickets to the concert.
   B：Oh, no. There are three of us who want to go to the concert.
   A：I will try to buy another one on the Internet.

Q：Where will he try to buy another ticket?

   a. On the phone.   c. At school.
   b. From her brother. d. On the Internet.

解説：three of us は直訳すると「私達のうち3人」となる。この内容だとコンサートに行きたい人は3人いるという事である。

Part 4　Short Talks／説明文問題

次の説明文の質問に最も適当な答えを選びなさい。

スエーデン

Sweden is a country in the part of Europe named Scandinavia. To the east of Sweden is the country of Finland. The capital city of Sweden is Stockholm. Swedish people eat a lot of fish, meat and potatoes. One of the most famous meals in the country is Swedish meatballs. The water in Sweden is very clean, and the nation has a very good health care system. Many people like to visit Sweden to see the beautiful coasts and nature.

1. Which country is to the east of Sweden?
   - a. Norway.
   - b. Finland.
   - c. France.
   - d. Scotland.

2. What is one of the most famous meals in Sweden?
   - a. Swedish coffee.
   - b. Swedish meatballs.
   - c. Swedish tacos.
   - d. Swedish apple pie.

解説：設問1　To the east of Sweden「スウェーデンの東には」に続く地名を答えればよい。To the east of Sweden is the country of Finland。

設問2　ここでもひっかけなしで One of the most famous meals in the country is「この国で最も有名な料理の1つは」に続く料理名が答えである。

ダイアモンド

Diamonds are beautiful gems. Many are clear, but some of them have colors, such as pink and yellow. Diamonds were first found in India but have been found in many countries today. They are very rare, so they are expensive to buy. It is a tradition in the U.S. that when people get married, the man buys a diamond ring for his wife.

1. Where were diamonds first found?
   - a. China.
   - b. The U.S.
   - c. India.
   - d. Africa.

2. What does a man buy for his wife when he gets married?
   - a. A diamond necklace.
   - b. A diamond ring.
   - c. A diamond box.
   - d. A diamond store.

解説：設問1　Diamonds were first found in India とある。First「最初に」という単語が入る場所に注意しよう。

設問2　アメリカ合衆国の伝統では、カップルが結婚する際に the man buys a diamond ring for his wife「男性が妻のためにダイヤモンドの指輪を買う」とある。日本でも婚約指輪はとくにダイヤモンドが入っているものが人気のようだ。

Part 5 Reading／読解演習

次の段落文を読み、各設問に対して最も適切な答えを選びなさい（各段落速読問題は2分以内に終わらせなさい）。

スピードリーディング

The Model T was the first model of automobile developed by Henry Ford in 1903. It sold for $830. His company, Ford Motors, was the first to use an assembly line. An assembly line is useful for companies because a large amount of items can be produced very quickly. Soon, cars were being driven to and from cities, and people relied on cars to get to places. Moreover, more jobs were created. Car-related businesses included repairing broken cars, washing cars, selling cars, and making accessories for the car. A lot has changed since 1903, but one thing remains: the demand for cars.

1. What was the first model developed by Ford?
    a. The Henry.   c. The Model T.
    b. The T.   d. The Ford Motor.

2. What helps a company produce large amounts of products?
    a. A car.   c. A Model T.
    b. Robots.   d. An assembly line.

Today, the average American purchases a new car every five or six years. So, in a lifetime, an American may own a dozen cars. There is approximately one car for every person in the United States, and the number of vehicles exceeds the number of licensed drivers. For many people, the car is a convenient type of transportation because it is fast and efficient. For others, car ownership is an enjoyable hobby, and collectors save money to buy new models. Whether it is for practical purposes or for a hobby, cars are a major part of the American lifestyle.

1. How often do Americans buy a car?
    a. Every year.   c. Every six months.
    b. Twelve times.   d. About every five years.

2. What does the number of cars outnumber?
    a. The amount of gas.   c. The number of teenage drivers.
    b. The number of licensed drivers.   d. The amount of time it takes to insure a car.

Some earth-friendly people believe that cars are bad for the environment since they pollute the air and use too much fuel. Rather than driving a car, these environmentalists recommend taking the bus or biking to places. However, they suggest that if you must take your car, then carpool with a few people to save gas and to reduce the pollution. Whereas some people are passionate about driving and collecting cars, there are people who see cars as problematic and harmful to the environment.

1. If you drive a car, what do environmentalists suggest?
    a. Carpool with other people.   c. Share a car with your neighbor.
    b. Put a bike in the back seat.   d. Wash it only once a month.

2. Why do some people think cars are problematic?
    a. Because they get too dirty.
    b. Because they cause traffic jams.
    c. Because they hurt the earth.
    d. Because they collect too many of them.

スピードリーディングと同じ文を読み、各設問に対して最も適切な答えを選びなさい。

読解問題

The Model T was the first model of automobile developed by Henry Ford in 1903. It sold for $830. His company, Ford Motors, was the first to use an assembly line. An assembly line is useful for companies because a large amount of items can be produced very quickly. Soon, cars were being driven to and from cities, and people relied on cars to get to places. Moreover, more jobs were created. Car-related businesses included repairing broken cars, washing cars, selling cars, and making accessories for the car. A lot has changed since 1903, but one thing remains: the demand for cars.

Today, the average American purchases a new car every five or six years. So, in a lifetime, an American may own a dozen cars. There is approximately one car for every person in the United States, and the number of vehicles exceeds the number of licensed drivers. For many people, the car is a convenient type of transportation because it is fast and efficient. For others, car ownership is an enjoyable hobby, and collectors save money to buy new models. Whether it is for practical purposes or for a hobby, cars are a major part of the American lifestyle.

Some earth-friendly people believe that cars are bad for the environment since they pollute the air and use too much fuel. Rather than driving a car, these environmentalists recommend taking the bus or biking to places. However, they suggest that if you must take your car, then carpool with a few people to save gas and to reduce the pollution. Whereas some people are passionate about driving and collecting cars, there are people who see cars as problematic and harmful to the environment.

One concern that arises is how much fuel is available. Gasoline is a limited natural resource, so what happens when we run out of gasoline? Some car companies are developing different types of transportation. For example, car companies in Korea, Japan, and the United States have been working on an electric car. The electric car does not require gasoline, it does not create pollution, and it is quiet. However, the drawback is that gasoline-powered cars are faster. The design of cars may change in the future, but their importance will remain.

Comprehension Questions

1. How did the car industry help the American economy?
    a. It reduced pollution.
    b. It let women drive.
    c. Everyone could buy a car because it was so cheap.
    d. There were more jobs and businesses.

2. Why are cars considered to be a part of the American lifestyle?
    a. Because people use them daily, and some people collect them.
    b. Because Henry Ford designed a car for the president.
    c. Because teenagers, adults, and the elderly can drive them.
    d. Because every American family owns a car.

3. What is one benefit of carpooling?

    a. You can meet new people.

    b. You can find a better parking space.

    c. You can take your car by the pool.

    d. You can save on gas.

4. What have some car companies been working on?

    a. A faster car than a gasoline-powered car.

    b. A car that does not need unleaded fuel.

    c. A car that does not require gas.

    d. A more affordable car.

Part 6　Error Recognition／誤文訂正問題

各文には文法的誤りがあります。訂正もしくは書き換えを必要とする語句を選びなさい。

1. Because <u>I'm having</u> a hard time paying the rent each month, I <u>should</u> spend <u>lesser</u> money <u>on</u> clothes.
   　　　　　A　　　　　　　　　　　　　　　　　　　　　　　　　　　B　　　　　　C　　　　　　D
   解説：「より少なく」という意味の「量」における比較級は less である。訳参照。
   正しい英文：Because I'm having a hard time paying the rent each month, I should spend less money on clothes.

2. He <u>haven't like</u> to <u>wake up</u> <u>early</u> in the morning. John is what my mother <u>calls</u> a night owl.
   　　　　A　　　　　　　B　　　　　C　　　　　　　　　　　　　　　　　　　　　　　　D
   解説：1 文目は不適切な否定文である。（注釈：night owl：夜更かしする人）
   正しい英文：He doesn't like to wake up early in the morning. John is what my mother calls a night owl.

3. My aunt <u>mistakenly</u> added sugar <u>rather</u> of salt to the chicken casserole. She <u>had to</u> throw <u>it</u> away and
   　　　　　　A　　　　　　　　　　B　　　　　　　　　　　　　　　　　　　　　　C　　　　　　D
   start over.
   解説：instead of ～：～の代わりに
   正しい英文：My aunt mistakenly added sugar instead of salt to the chicken casserole. She had to throw it away and start over.

4. <u>Anyone</u> <u>stole</u> my purse when I was on vacation. I <u>couldn't</u> go shopping, and I <u>had to stay</u> in a cheap motel.
   　　A　　　　B　　　　　　　　　　　　　　　　　　　　C　　　　　　　　　　　　　　D
   解説：肯定文で用いられる anyone は「誰でも」と考える。よって、不可。someone（誰か）が適切となる。
   正しい英文：Someone stole my purse when I was on vacation. I couldn't go shopping, and I had to stay in a cheap motel.

5. If Jim <u>hadn't fixed</u> it, we <u>would have had</u> to pay a plumber. Thankfully, Uncle Jim repaired the pipe <u>to keep</u>
   　　　　　A　　　　　　　　B　　　　　　　　　　　　　　　　　　　　　　　　　　　　　　　　　　　C
   it from <u>leak</u>.
   　　　　　D
   解説：keep O from -ing：O が～するのを防ぐ（＝prevent O from -ing）
   正しい英文：If Jim hadn't fixed it, we would have had to pay a plumber. Thankfully, Uncle Jim repaired the pipe to keep it from leaking.

6. Don't <u>leave</u> your dirty <u>towel's</u> on the floor. Pick <u>them</u> up and put them in the <u>laundry</u> room.
   　　　　A　　　　　　　　　B　　　　　　　　　　　　C　　　　　　　　　　　　　　　　D
   解説：下線 B の語は、複数形名詞であることが適切。よって、towels が下線 B におかれる適切な語となる。
   正しい英文：Don't leave your dirty towels on the floor. Pick them up and put them in the laundry room.

7. Rachael is not coming to the party at 6:00 although she is working until 7:00. I'm sure she'll stop by on
                    A   B   C
her way home.
      D

解説：文脈から、下線 B には接続詞 because が適切である。訳参照。

正しい英文：Rachael is not coming to the party at 6:00 because she is working until 7:00. I'm sure she'll stop by on her way home.

Part 7 Incomplete Sentence／文法・語彙問題

文法的に適切な語句を1つ選び、文を完成させなさい。

1. Kurt bought flowers for his girlfriend. He is going to _____ at dinner.
    a. them give her   c. give them to her
    b. her to give them   d. her them give

    訳：カートは彼女に花を買った。彼は、夕食でそれらを彼女にあげるつもりだ。
    解説：意味の通る語順は c. give them to her である。訳参照。give A to B：A を B にあげる（＝give B A）

2. The number thirteen is considered _____ number.
    a. a mislucky   c. a disluck
    b. an exlucky   d. an unlucky

    訳：13番は不運な番号と考えられている。
    解説：d. an unlucky 以外の選択肢は存在しない語である。

3. My boyfriend is a football player, but _____ you and me, I don't care for the sport.
    a. between   c. with
    b. during   d. while

    訳：私のボーイフレンド兄（弟）はフットボール選手だが、ここだけの話、私はそのスポーツ（フットボール）が好きではになく、興味がない。
    解説：between you and me：ここだけの話だが

4. This fur coat _____ to me. Take good care of it.
    a. belonging   c. has belonged
    b. belongs   d. belong

    訳：この毛皮のコートは私のものです。丁寧に扱ってください。
    解説：動詞 belong は状態を表す動詞であるため、通例、原形のまま用いる。belong to：〜に属する

5. Bruce talks as if he _____ everything, but I don't think he's very smart.
    a. is knowing   c. known
    b. had known   d. knows

    訳：ブルースは、あたかもすべて知っているかのように話すが、彼はそんなに頭がよいとは思わない。
    解説：動詞 know は状態を表す動詞であるため、通例進行形にはしない。また、上の文では「現在」について述べられているため、現在形である d. knows が空欄に入る最も適切な語である。訳参照。

Lesson 11 （http://audio.lincenglish.com にアクセスして音声を聞いてください）

Part 1　Image Listening／写真描写問題

1. 左の写真を見て、人物の行動や物の位置などについて文を3つ作りなさい。
　_____
　_____
　_____

2. 写真の描写文として最も適切な文をA～Dの中から選びなさい。
　(A)，(B)，(C)，(D)

1. 左の写真を見て、人物の行動や物の位置などについて文を3つ作りなさい。
　_____
　_____
　_____

2. 写真の描写文として最も適切な文をA～Dの中から選びなさい。
　(A)，(B)，(C)，(D)

1. 左の写真を見て、人物の行動や物の位置などについて文を3つ作りなさい。
　_____
　_____
　_____

2. 写真の描写文として最も適切な文をA～Dの中から選びなさい。
　(A)，(B)，(C)，(D)

1. 左の写真を見て、人物の行動や物の位置などについて文を3つ作りなさい。
　_____
　_____
　_____

2. 写真の描写文として最も適切な文をA～Dの中から選びなさい。
　(A)，(B)，(C)，(D)

Part 2 Question and Response／質疑応答問題

重要な質問表現

Do you ever fight with your brother?
　　　fight は「争い」、またはささいな「喧嘩」としても使われる。
How did you do on the test?
　　　試験がどうだったか、自分が試験でよくできたかどうかなどを答える。
When will you come over?
　　　come over「〜へやってくる」。
Why don't you take off your coat?
　　　take off「脱ぐ」。
Who can carry my bags for me?
　　　「誰」が手伝ってくれるのか。
Why did she go to the hair salon?
　　　美容院に行く主な目的は単純に「髪を切る」ためと考えるのが適当である。
Which is faster, the train or the bus?
　　　比べているのは電車とバスの「かかる時間」である。
Could you please pass the salt?
　　　質問文はそのまま使えるので覚えておこう。
What is the dog looking at?
　　　犬が見ているものは何か。
Should I stop at the store on my way home?
　　　stop at「〜に立ち寄る」、on my way home「家に帰る途中」。

確認ドリル

次の1〜5の質問に対して最も適切な応答をそれぞれ（A）〜（C）の中から選びなさい。

1. Why did you quit your job?
   (A)　Because I work at a doctor's office.
   (B)　Because I found a better job.
   (C)　Because my boss is very nice.

2. Why didn't you come to class yesterday?
   (A)　I wasn't feeling well.
   (B)　I have my homework.
   (C)　I am 17 years old.

3. What is your favorite holiday?
   (A)　My family eats a lot of food on holidays.
   (B)　I like the Thanksgiving holiday the most.
   (C)　Every country has different holidays.

4. Did you turn off the television?
   (A)　Yes, my favorite program was over.
   (B)　No, I turned it on already.
   (C)　I don't like to watch TV.

5. How long have you been an author?
   (A)　For ten years.
   (B)　I saw it ten years ago.
   (C)　The man is an artist.

Part 3 Short Conversation／会話問題

次の会話を読んで、質問に最も適当な答えを選びなさい。

質問文パターン

* Where 型パターン

1. **A**：I am looking for a book about cats.
   B：We have many books about cats for sale. Here is one you will like.
   A：Thank you. I'd like to buy it.

   Q：Where are the speakers?
     a. At the grocery store. c. At a bookstore.
     b. In the classroom. d. At the library.

   解説：本を探している様子から「本屋」にいると予想がつく。

* Why 型パターン

2. **A**：Do you have a pet dog or cat?
   B：I have a dog. I love cats, but I am allergic to them.
   A：Oh, that's too bad.

   Q：Why doesn't he have a cat?
     a. Because he is allergic to them. c. Because he is afraid of them.
     b. Because he doesn't like them. d. Because he thinks they are dirty.

   解説：猫は好きだがアレルギーがあるという。

* Who 型パターン

3. **A**：That dinner was great! Did your mother teach you how to cook?
   B：No, my grandmother taught me how to cook.
   A：Well, she did a great job!

   Q：Who taught him how to cook?
     a. His father. c. His mother.
     b. His grandfather. d. His grandmother.

   解説：料理を教えたのは母ではなく、祖母である。

* What 型パターン

4. **A**：Do you have a computer at your house?
   B：Yes. My family has high-speed Internet.
   A：Let's go to your house and download some music.

Q：What does he want to do on the Internet?
- a. Play a game.
- b. Check email.
- c. Find information.
- d. Download music.

解説：会話文最後がそのまま正解につながる。

Part 4 Short Talks ／説明文問題

次の説明文の質問に最も適当な答えを選びなさい。

トンネル

A tunnel is a space that allows people to travel under the ground, mountains or water. Some tunnels are used for cars, and other tunnels are for trains. The Channel Tunnel is a very long tunnel. It is 50 kilometers long, and it lets people travel by train from France to England. The largest tunnel in the world is in Switzerland.

1. Why do people use tunnels?
   - a. To see the mountains.
   - b. To take a walk.
   - c. To travel.
   - d. To see the ocean.

2. Where is the largest tunnel?
   - a. France.
   - b. England.
   - c. Sweden.
   - d. Switzerland.

解説：設問1　トンネルはどういうものかという説明で allows people to travel under the ground, mountains or water.「人びとが地下、山の下、そして水面下を移動できるようにする」とある。Travel という単語には「旅行」という意味だけでなく、「移動する」などという意味もあることに注意。

設問2　本文最後の文に、世界一長いトンネルは is in Switzerland である「スイスにある」とある。

ワイン

Wine is an alcoholic drink that is made from the juice of grapes. There are two main types of wine, red wine and white wine. People began making wine more than 6,000 years ago. The countries that drink the most wine are France, Italy, Argentina and the U.S.

1. What are the two main types of wine?
   - a. Red and black.
   - b. White and black.
   - c. Red and white.
   - d. Grape.

2. How long ago did people begin to make wine?
   - a. 6,000 years.
   - b. 10,000 years.
   - c. 9,000 years.
   - d. 600 years.

解説：設問1　ワインの主な種類は red wine「赤ワイン」と white wine「白ワイン」である。

設問2　人びとがワインを作り出したのは more than 6,000 years ago「6,000年以上前」である。More than「～以上」の対義語は less than「～以下」である。

Part 5　Reading／読解演習

次の段落文を読み、各設問に対して最も適切な答えを選びなさい（各段落速読問題は2分以内に終わらせなさい）。

スピードリーディング

　Maps have been around for centuries, and they are a useful tool for people to navigate new places. In fact, astrologers used them to plot the planets in the solar system. Archeologists found some maps in Iraq that are over 4,300 years old. Although modern map users rely on the Internet or a print-out of a map, the maps discovered in Iraq were made of clay. In China, there were maps made of silk that date back 2,000 years ago. Maps come in several shapes, sizes, and materials, but they continue to be an important part of living.

　　1. What did astrologers use maps for?
　　　　a. To draw the planets.　　c. To make new tools.
　　　　b. To find the moon.　　　d. To navigate in the sea.

　　2. What were the maps found in Iraq made of?
　　　　a. Paper.　　c. Silk.
　　　　b. Clay.　　　d. Wood.

　The first map of the world may have been created in Babylonia, which is present day Iraq. This map, which is 2,600 years old, was not very accurate. The people did not know what the world looked like, but some of their ideas were drawn on the map. For example, the Babylonian map represented earth as being flat, not round. Rather than having continents, the map had one ocean with several smaller islands within it. Other maps dating back to this time have earth on the back of a large turtle. Beneath the turtle, there are four elephants holding up the earth. An ancient myth said that if any of the animals moved, then the earth would move and shake. As a result, an earthquake would occur.

　　1. What did the earth look like on the Babylonian map?
　　　　a. The earth was flat.　　　c. The earth only had one continent.
　　　　b. The earth was round.　　d. They earth was smaller than the moon.

　　2. According to myth, what was below the turtle on the map of the earth?
　　　　a. An earthquake.　　c. Elephants.
　　　　b. An elephant.　　　d. The moon.

　For centuries, people thought the earth was flat, and they were not able to determine the size of the earth. It wasn't until the third century that scientists realized the earth was a sphere, and not flat. A Greek scholar named Eratosthenes used the sun and geometry to measure the size of the earth. Eratosthenes concluded that the circumference of the earth was about 28,000 miles, and he was not too far off from the true measurement, which is 25,000 miles. Although there were many maps of Asia, Europe, and north Africa, people did not know much about other parts of the world. People began to explore and draw maps as they went to new places.

1. When did people find out the earth was a sphere?
    a. In the 1800s.
    b. In the fifth century.
    c. In the third century.
    d. In 300 B.C.

2. What did Eratosthenes use to measure the size of earth?
    a. A map and a calculator.
    b. The sun and math.
    c. A ruler and the position of the sun.
    d. The sun and the moon.

スピードリーディングと同じ文を読み、各設問に対して最も適切な答えを選びなさい。

読解問題

Maps have been around for centuries, and they are a useful tool for people to navigate new places. In fact, astrologers used them to plot the planets in the solar system. Archeologists found some maps in Iraq that are over 4,300 years old. Although modern map users rely on the Internet or a print-out of a map, the maps discovered in Iraq were made of clay. In China, there were maps made of silk that date back 2,000 years ago. Maps come in several shapes, sizes, and materials, but they continue to be an important part of living.

The first map of the world may have been created in Babylonia, which is present day Iraq. This map, which is 2,600 years old, was not very accurate. The people did not know what the world looked like, but some of their ideas were drawn on the map. For example, the Babylonian map represented earth as being flat, not round. Rather than having continents, the map had one ocean with several smaller islands within it. Other maps dating back to this time have earth on the back of a large turtle. Beneath the turtle, there are four elephants holding up the earth. An ancient myth said that if any of the animals moved, then the earth would move and shake. As a result, an earthquake would occur.

For centuries, people thought the earth was flat, and they were not able to determine the size of the earth. It wasn't until the third century that scientists realized the earth was a sphere, and not flat. A Greek scholar named Eratosthenes used the sun and geometry to measure the size of the earth. Eratosthenes concluded that the circumference of the earth was about 28,000 miles, and he was not too far off from the true measurement, which is 25,000 miles. Although there were many maps of Asia, Europe, and north Africa, people did not know much about other parts of the world. People began to explore and draw maps as they went to new places.

Many experts believe that the ancient maps show that people were moving forward and were thinking about new places. People learned more about places as well as people with the use of maps. Map makers, known as cartographers, drew correct maps of countries around Europe in the eighteenth and nineteenth centuries. However, the first true maps of the world were not made until the late 1800s. Since then, many inventions have been made to help make maps easier to draw. The printing press, the telescope, and the underwater camera have helped in the development of maps. Today's maps are very advanced and accurate, but there is still a lot of land and water to explore.

Comprehension Questions

1. Why do you think maps were made of silk in China?
    a. Because the Chinese did not like the color of clay.
    b. Because it was strong material and lasted a long time.
    c. Because it looked prettier.
    d. Because it was easy to draw on and water did not hurt it.

2. On the Babylonian map, how many continents did the earth have?
    a. Seven continents, but America was very small.
    b. Three continents—Europe, Asia, and Africa.
    c. Only one.
    d. None. It had islands instead.

3. Where was Eratosthenes from?
    a. Asia.
    b. North Africa.
    c. Greece.
    d. Germany.

4. According to some experts, what do maps represent about people?
    a. People liked to draw.
    b. People were advancing their way of life.
    c. People did not know the earth was round until 1900.
    d. People spent eight hours a day making maps.

Part 6　Error Recognition／誤文訂正問題

各文には文法的誤りがあります。訂正もしくは書き換えを必要とする語句を選びなさい。

1. I <u>am supposing</u> I <u>could go</u> to the movie on Friday. Is it just you and <u>I</u> going, or are <u>we</u> going with a group?
　　　　A　　　　　　　　B　　　　　　　　　　　　　　　　　　　　　　C　　　　　　　　　D

　解説：動詞 suppose（〜について考える）は状態を表す動詞であるため、通例進行形にはしない。

　正しい英文：I suppose I could go to the movie on Friday. Is it just you and I going, or are we going with a group?

2. I don't think <u>that</u> I will <u>ever</u> leave this beautiful place. I <u>been living</u> here <u>since</u> 2004.
　　　　　　　　A　　　　　　B　　　　　　　　　　　　　　　　C　　　　　　　　D

　解説：下線Bの動詞句は不完全な現在完了進行形（have（has）been ＋過去分詞）。よって、have been living が下線Cに置かれる適切な動詞句となる。

　正しい英文：I don't think that I will ever leave this beautiful place. I have been living here since 2004.

3. My mom <u>has been</u> talking <u>for</u> that book all week. She just finished <u>reading</u> it, and she absolutely loved <u>it</u>.
　　　　　　　A　　　　　　　　B　　　　　　　　　　　　　　　　　　　　C　　　　　　　　　　　　　　　　D

　解説：意味内容的に、下線Bに置かれる前置詞は about（〜について）が適切である。talk about 〜：〜について話す

　正しい英文：My mom has been talking about that book all week. She just finished reading it, and she absolutely loved it.

4. This is the <u>second times</u> that <u>I've been</u> to Georgia. My first time was <u>when</u> I was three years old, so that
　　　　　　　　A　　　　　　　　B　　　　　　　　　　　　　　　　　　　　C

really <u>doesn't count</u>.
　　　　D

　解説：「回数」を表す time は複数形にはしない。

　正しい英文：This is the second time that I've been to Georgia. My first time was when I was three years old, so that really doesn't count.

5. <u>Sometimes</u> my brothers don't know the answers to my questions. When <u>they</u> answer me, I don't always
　　　A　　　　　　　　　　　　　　　　　　　　　　　　　　　　　　　　　　　　　B

believe what <u>them</u> say <u>to me</u>.
　　　　　　　　C　　　　　D

　解説：下線Cの語は主格を取るため they であることが適切である。

　正しい英文：Sometimes my brothers don't know the answers to my questions. When they answer me, I don't always believe what they say to me.

6. <u>Instead</u> than playing golf, <u>let's go</u> swimming tomorrow. We <u>haven't been</u> to the beach <u>since</u> last summer.
　　　A　　　　　　　　　　　　　　B　　　　　　　　　　　　　　　　　　C　　　　　　　　　　　　　　D

　解説：rather than 〜：〜するよりも（注釈：A is B rather than C：A は C というよりむしろ B だ）

　正しい英文：Rather than playing golf, let's go swimming tomorrow. We haven't been to the beach since last summer.

7. Do you know <u>why</u> Martha <u>won't she</u> go to the concert <u>with us</u>? Is she <u>still</u> mad at Carl?
      A   B   C   D

 解説：下線 B の語から she を取れば文章の意味が通る。訳参照。

 正しい英文：Do you know why Martha won't go to the concert with us? Is she still mad at Carl?

Part 7 Incomplete Sentence／文法・語彙問題

文法的に適切な語句を1つ選び、文を完成させなさい。

1. Do you want _____ front of the station at 6:00?
    a. meeting in   c. to meet at
    b. to meeting at   d. to meet in

訳：駅前で6時に会う？
解説：want to 不定詞：〜したい　in front of 〜：〜の前で

2. They _____ to go to the Gap since yesterday. Maybe we should go shopping.
    a. have wanting   c. have been wanting
    b. been wanted   d. have been wanted

訳：彼らは昨日からギャップに行きたがっている。おそらく、ショッピングに行くべきだね。
解説：文脈より、過去のある1点から事柄が現在まで継続している「現在完了進行形（have（has）been -ing）」が空欄に入る適切な動詞句だと推測できる。よって、c. have been wanting が空欄に入る最も適切な語となる。また、残りの選択肢はすべて、文法的に不適切である。

3. Besides Gloria, does anybody _____ want to go to the movies?
    a. other   c. either
    b. else   d. too

訳：グロリア以外に、誰か他に映画に行きたい人はいますか？
解説：文脈より、b. else が空欄に入る最も適切な語である。anybody else：他の誰か

4. I was going to open another program, but I already had three programs _____.
    a. doing   c. surfing
    b. registering d. running

訳：もう1つプログラムを開けるつもりだったが、すでに3つのプログラムを作動させていた。
解説：文脈より、d. running が空欄に入る最も適切な語である。have O -ing：Oを〜させる　run（自）：作動する（注釈：register：〜を登録する　surf：サーフィンする）

5. Every six months, I go to the dentist and get a _____.
    a. check out   c. check up
    b. check-in   d. check on

訳：6か月おきに、私は歯医者へ行き、診察してもらう。
解説：文脈より、名詞 check up（点検・医療診断）が空欄に入る最も適切な語である。

110

Lesson 12 （http://audio.lincenglish.com にアクセスして音声を聞いてください）

Part 1　Image Listening／写真描写問題

1. 左の写真を見て、人物の行動や物の位置などについて文を3つ作りなさい。
   _____
   _____
   _____

2. 写真の描写文として最も適切な文をA〜Dの中から選びなさい。
   (A), (B), (C), (D)

1. 左の写真を見て、人物の行動や物の位置などについて文を3つ作りなさい。
   _____
   _____
   _____

2. 写真の描写文として最も適切な文をA〜Dの中から選びなさい。
   (A), (B), (C), (D)

1. 左の写真を見て、人物の行動や物の位置などについて文を3つ作りなさい。
   _____
   _____
   _____

2. 写真の描写文として最も適切な文をA〜Dの中から選びなさい。
   (A), (B), (C), (D)

1. 左の写真を見て、人物の行動や物の位置などについて文を3つ作りなさい。
   _____
   _____
   _____

2. 写真の描写文として最も適切な文をA〜Dの中から選びなさい。
   (A), (B), (C), (D)

Part 2 Question and Response／質疑応答問題

重要な質問表現

How many days until your new job begins?
　　until「〜まで」を聞き取れれば正解につながる。

Where can I find the bus station?
　　バス停の位置を尋ねている。

Who is that guy over there?
　　「誰」をきかれているのであって「何をしているのか」「その人の経験」をきかれているのではない。

Who can give me a ride to the store?
　　give one a ride「(人を) 車に乗せる」。

Do you know where I can find the library?
　　図書館がどういうところかの説明ではなく、場所の説明をしなければならない。

When did you arrive in Japan?
　　日本に着いた「日時」を答える。

How many people are in your class?
　　クラスの人数をきかれている。

Have you seen a camel before?
　　a camel「ラクダ」を見たことがあるかどうかの経験の有無を答える。

Who called you last night?
　　「誰が」電話をかけてきたか。(誰に) かけたかではないことに注意しよう。

Who will pay the bills?
　　bill「請求書」を「誰」が払うのか。

確認ドリル

次の1〜5の質問に対して最も適切な応答をそれぞれ (A)〜(C) の中から選びなさい。

1. What time will Dad get home?
   (A) Yes, he is at work.
   (B) He will be home soon.
   (C) We will talk later.

2. Where are the sandwiches I made?
   (A) I put them in the refrigerator.
   (B) Let's go to the restaurant.
   (C) Here is some juice.

3. Did Katie call?
   (A) Here she is.
   (B) Yes, she left this message for you.
   (C) Yes, she is your friend.

4. Do you have any money?
   (A) No, I'm broke.
   (B) This store is expensive.
   (C) Let's go to the movie.

5. Could I borrow the car?
   (A) Only if you take good care of it.
   (B) She is tired.
   (C) The car is red.

Part 3　Short Conversation／会話問題

次の会話を読んで、質問に最も適当な答えを選びなさい。

質問文パターン

* Who 型パターン

1. **A**：My favorite band is the Beatles.
   B：Oh, yes! I love that song "Let It Be."
   A：Me too. I learned it in school to practice my English.

   Q：Who sings the song, "Let It Be"?
   　　　a. The Beatles.　　　c. The Boxcars.
   　　　b. The Blue Men.　　d. The Band.

   解説："Let it be" は人気イギリスバンドの「ビートルズ」が歌っている。

* Where 型パターン

2. **A**：Ryan, where is your car?
   B：I parked my car over there, next to the tree.
   A：Oh, I see it!

   Q：Where did Ryan park his car?
   　　　a. Next to the school.　　c. Next to the bank.
   　　　b. Next to the tree.　　　d. Next to the library.

   解説：park「駐車する」。車を駐車したのは「何」の隣か。

* What 型パターン

3. **A**：Let's go dancing tonight.
   B：O.K. Where do you want to go?
   A：I would like to go to the club.

   Q：What do they want to do?
   　　　a. Go dancing.　　　c. Work.
   　　　b. Go swimming.　　d. Study.

   解説：彼らの行き先は「(踊るための) クラブ」である。

* When 型パターン

4. **A**：I hope you will come to visit me soon.
   B：I plan to visit you in two months.
   A：Good! I miss you!

Q：When does he plan to visit her?
   a. Tomorrow. c. In two days.
   b. In a year.   d. In two months.

解説：in two months「2 か月以内に」。前置詞 in の用法を再確認しよう。

Part 4　Short Talks ／説明文問題

次の説明文の質問に最も適当な答えを選びなさい。

ピーチ

Peaches are a delicious, healthy fruit first found in China. Peaches are usually orange or white. They taste very sweet, and people often eat peaches in desserts, like peach pie. Sometimes people eat peaches with milk. Peaches grow on trees and have a stone in the center, called a "pit." The peach is the most popular fruit in the state of Georgia, in the southern United States.

1. Where were peaches first found?
   - a. The United States.
   - b. China.
   - c. India.
   - d. France.

2. In what state in the U.S. are peaches the most popular fruit?
   - a. Georgia.
   - b. California.
   - c. Florida.
   - d. Texas.

解説：設問1　冒頭文に first found in China「中国で最初に発見された」とある。
　　　設問2　アメリカ合衆国南東部の州にはアトランタオリンピックが開催された都市、アトランタなどがある。ジョージア州のニックネームが peach state「桃の州」とされるほど桃が人気のようだ。

睡眠時間

It is very important to get enough sleep. The average person needs about eight hours of sleep every night. Babies need more sleep than this and often sleep several times during the day in addition to sleeping at night. The reason for sleeping is so that the body can rest and so people feel good in the morning. If people do not get enough sleep, they may feel tired, angry or nervous. If you have a big test at school in the morning, make sure you get a good night's sleep!

1. How much sleep does an average person need?
   - a. Five hours.
   - b. Eight hours.
   - c. Six hours.
   - d. Two hours.

2. What should you do if you have a big test in the morning?
   - a. Get a lot of sleep.
   - b. Stay awake all night.
   - c. Rest.
   - d. Get angry.

解説：設問1　about eight hours of sleep「8時間ほどの睡眠」とある。必要な睡眠時間は人によって違うが、大抵は最低8時間の睡眠が必要と言われている。
　　　設問2　If you have a big test at school in the morning、「朝に大きい試験が学校であるのなら」make sure you get a good night's sleep!「良い睡眠を取るように努めましょう！」とある。Make sure「確かめる、確認する」。

Part 5 Reading／読解演習

次の段落文を読み、各設問に対して最も適切な答えを選びなさい（各段落速読問題は 2 分以内に終わらせなさい）。

スピードリーディング

When children are growing up, they usually play in same-sex groups. Boys love competition, and they usually play physical sports with a group of males their age. When they use their imagination, it often involves guns, weapons, and being a leader. In class, many boys like to get attention by talking loudly or telling all the other classmates about a good grade. In contrast, girls do not care as much about winning, but they do want to be liked by other girls. In addition, girls often play in smaller groups and sometimes play only with one "best friend." Girls like to play fairly, and they do not talk out as much in class or be the "class clown" as much as boys. The gender of a person, which means being either male or female, is a basic part of a person's identity.

1. Girls do not care about winning, but what do they care about?
    a. Being liked by other girls.   c. Getting the highest grade in class.
    b. Being liked by other boys.   d. Going to sports practice after school.

2. What does "gender" mean?
    a. Being the best in the class.   c. Being either male or female.
    b. Having general ideas about life. d. Playing fairly with other girls.

The differences in the way boys and girls behave, think, and talk are learned when they are very young. Parents often buy blue colored presents or gifts that represent masculinity for boys. For example, boys play with guns, trucks, and toy soldiers when they are young. Parents often buy girls pink colored presents or gifts that represent femininity. For instance, girls play with dolls, houses, and with clothing for "dress-up." As children grow up, their gender will affect their decision-making and their behavior with other people. Male teenagers will gain respect by their accomplishments in sports and by showing their knowledge. Female teenagers will gain respect by having popular friends. Gender plays an important role throughout life.

1. What do parents often buy boys?
    a. Blue, black, and red colored presents.   c. Masculine gifts, such as trucks.
    b. Feminine gifts, such as guns.   d. Anything the boys ask for.

2. How will female teenagers get respect from other people?
    a. By being smart.   c. By playing sports.
    b. By having popular friends.   d. By talking to older boys.

As adults, men and women sometimes have a difficult time communicating to each other. When a married woman talks to her husband about a problem, she expects him to listen and to offer ways to help. She may feel upset if he gives a direct, logical answer without showing too much emotion. A female boss may talk differently to her employees than a male boss would because she grew up with different styles of talking and communicating than a male. Also, many studies show that men, in general, are more analytical and logical than women. Women, on the other hand, are more sensitive and emotion-based. The differences in the way men and women think can balance a workplace, but it can also create stress and tension.

1. According to the reading, when might a wife feel upset with her husband?
   a. When the husband comes home late from work.
   b. When the husband buys her a blue colored present.
   c. When the husband is logical and direct.
   d. When the husband shows a lot of emotion.

2. What did the study show about women?
   a. They are logical and emotional.
   b. They are shy and sensitive.
   c. They are very direct and honest.
   d. They are emotional and sensitive.

スピードリーディングと同じ文を読み、各設問に対して最も適切な答えを選びなさい。

読解問題

When children are growing up, they usually play in same-sex groups. Boys love competition, and they usually play physical sports with a group of males their age. When they use their imagination, it often involves guns, weapons, and being a leader. In class, many boys like to get attention by talking loudly or telling all the other classmates about a good grade. In contrast, girls do not care as much about winning, but they do want to be liked by other girls. In addition, girls often play in smaller groups and sometimes play only with one "best friend." Girls like to play fairly, and they do not talk out as much in class or be the "class clown" as much as boys. The gender of a person, which means being either male or female, is a basic part of a person's identity.

The differences in the way boys and girls behave, think, and talk are learned when they are very young. Parents often buy blue colored presents or gifts that represent masculinity for boys. For example, boys play with guns, trucks, and toy soldiers when they are young. Parents often buy girls pink colored presents or gifts that represent femininity. For instance, girls play with dolls, houses, and with clothing for "dress-up." As children grow up, their gender will affect their decision-making and their behavior with other people. Male teenagers will gain respect by their accomplishments in sports and by showing their knowledge. Female teenagers will gain respect by having popular friends. Gender plays an important role throughout life.

As adults, men and women sometimes have a difficult time communicating to each other. When a married woman talks to her husband about a problem, she expects him to listen and to offer ways to help. She may feel upset if he gives a direct, logical answer without showing too much emotion. A female boss may talk differently to her employees than a male boss would because she grew up with different styles of talking and communicating than a male. Also, many studies show that men, in general, are more analytical and logical than women. Women, on the other hand, are more sensitive and emotion-based. The differences in the way men and women think can balance a workplace, but it can also create stress and tension.

Gender also affects how males and females define friendship. Most American men think that friendships mean doing things together, such as going fishing or playing soccer. The act of doing an activity is more important than talking. In contrast, most American women consider a good friend as someone with whom they talk to on a frequent basis. Women's friendships are based on talking and having similar tastes, whereas men's friendships are based on activities. Some people also think that it is very difficult for men and women to have an "only friendship" relationship with each other. One psychologist explained, "There are too many emotions involved for a man and a woman to only be friends. Even if it is not spoken, either the male or the female has stronger feelings than just friendship toward the other person." Gender is an important part of every culture, and men and women behave differently, with different cultural rules, in every culture.

Comprehension Questions

1. Who do girls usually play with when they are young?
    a. A mix of boys and girls.
    b. Their neighbor after school, until their parents get home.
    c. A large group of girls their age or older.
    d. Other girls, usually a small group.

2. Why do parents often buy dolls and pretty clothes for their daughter?
    a. Because it is a sign of masculinity.
    b. Because they are not expensive.
    c. Because girls would never play with trucks.
    d. Because it is a sign of femininity.

3. What can happen when men and women work together?
    a. It can cause more problems without any good solutions.
    b. It can make the people work later because of communication difficulties.
    c. It can cause stress, but it can also create balance.
    d. It can help people who don't have same-sex friends.

4. According to the psychologist, why can't men and women be "only friends"?
    a. Men usually feel superior to women.
    b. There are a lot of different emotions between men and women.
    c. Women don't like to do as many activities as men.
    d. Women like to talk a lot, but men prefer not to talk very much.

Part 6　Error Recognition ／誤文訂正問題

各文には文法的誤りがあります。訂正もしくは書き換えを必要とする語句を選びなさい。

1. While I was driving, another car hit my rear bumper. Fortunately, none got hurt.
　　　　　　　　　　　　　　A　　　　　B　　　　　　　　　　　　　　C　　　　D

    解説：none は代名詞であり、それを指す対象が文章内に無いため不適切である。

    正しい英文：While I was driving, another car hit my rear bumper. Fortunately, no one got hurt.

2. I wish the sun would come out. The weather been awful for the past two weeks.
　　　　　　　　　　　　　　A　　　　　　　　　　　B　　C　　　　　D

    解説：2文目が不完全な現在完了形（have（has）＋過去分詞）の文章であることに注意しよう。

    正しい英文：I wish the sun would come out. The weather has been awful for the past two weeks.

3. Few of the clients were able to attend the luncheon. Most of they had meetings to attend.
　　　A　　　　　　　　　　　　　B　　　　　　　　　　　C　　　D

    解説：下線Dの語は前置詞 of の目的語となるため、目的格 them であることが適切である。

    正しい英文：Few of the clients were able to attend the luncheon. Most of them had meetings to attend.

4. The room was as hot as a desert. I began to feel dizziness, so I had to sit down.
　　　　　　　　　A　　　　　　　　　　B　　　　　　C　　　　　　　　D

    解説：feel ＋形：〜と感じる

    正しい英文：The room was as hot as a desert. I began to feel dizzy, so I had to sit down.

    正しい英文の訳：その部屋は砂漠のように暑い。目まいがしてきたので、座らなければならなかった。

5. Ron just talked to his boss. He is not feeling well, and he is wanting to go home early today.
　　　　　A　　　　　　　　　　　　　　　　　　　B　　　　　　　C　　　　　　　　　　D

    解説：want は状態を表す動詞であるため、通例進行形にはしない。

    正しい英文：Ron just talked to his boss. He is not feeling well, and he wants to go home early today.

6. The author's previous novel was a huge success. In fact, over one million copies were sold. He is current
　　　　　　　　　A　　　　　　　　　　　　　B　　　　　　　　　　　　　　　　　　　C　　　　　　D

    working on a new novel.

    解説：意味内容的に、下線Dの語はその後に続く動詞を修飾している副詞であることが適切。よって、副詞 currently（現在）が適切となる。current（現在の）は形容詞である。

    正しい英文：The author's previous novel was a huge success. In fact, over one million copies were sold. He is currently working on a new novel.

7. I'll be seeing you at the office on Tuesday. My flight gets in late on Monday night, so I'll probably be jet-
　　　　　　A　　　　　　　　　　　　　　　　　　　　B　　　　　　　　　　　　　　C　　　　D

    lagged and tired.

    解説：1文目において、意味内容的に、人と別れたり、電話を切る時に用いられる I'll see you（またね）という表現がここでは自然である。訳参照。

    正しい英文：I'll see you at the office on Tuesday. My flight gets in late on Monday night, so I'll probably be jet-lagged and tired.

Part 7　Incomplete Sentence／文法・語彙問題

文法的に適切な語句を1つ選び、文を完成させなさい。

1. What they are talking about has _____ to do with you.
    - a. any
    - b. anything
    - c. none
    - d. nothing

    訳：彼らが話していることはあなたとは何も関係がない。
    解説：have（has）nothing to do with 〜：〜と何も関係がない（注釈：have（has）something to do with 〜：〜と何か関係がある）

2. It has been so dry here lately. _____, it hasn't rained for at least 40 days.
    - a. Mostly
    - b. Considering
    - c. To prove
    - d. In fact

    訳：近頃、ここはとても乾燥している。実際、少なくとも40日間雨が降っていない。
    解説：文脈より、d. in fact（実際）が空欄に入る最も適切な語である。

3. There was a fifteen minute intermission _____ the play. I got up and stretched my legs.
    - a. throughout
    - b. among
    - c. during
    - d. into

    訳：演技の間、15分の休憩があった。私は起きて、足を伸ばした。
    解説：文脈より、前置詞 c. during（〜の間）が空欄に入る最も適切な語である。（注釈：a. throughout（前）：〜の至る所に）

4. When did you first hear _____ the video game?
    - a. at
    - b. about
    - c. with
    - d. on

    訳：初めてそのテレビゲームについて聞いたのはいつですか？
    解説：意味内容的に、前置詞 b. about が空欄に入る最も適切な語である。hear about：〜について聞く

5. Do you _____ if I ask you a personal question?
    - a. bother
    - b. mind
    - c. wonder
    - d. suggest

    訳：個人的な質問をしていいですか？
    解説：Do（would）you mind if SV：Sが〜してもいいですか？

解　答

Lesson 1

Part 1　Image Listening:
1. B
2. C
3. C
4. B

Part 2　Question and Response: Drills:
1. C
2. A
3. C
4. B
5. C

Part 3　Short Conversation:
1. B
2. B
3. D
4. A

Part 4　Short Talks:
First paragraph:
1. D
2. A
Second paragraph:
1. B
2. D

Part 5　Speed Reading:
First paragraph:
1. D
2. B
Second paragraph:
1. D
2. A
Third paragraph:
1. C
2. A
Comprehension Questions:
1. C
2. B
3. D
4. B

Part 6　Error Recognition:
1. C
2. D
3. C
4. D
5. A
6. D
7. D

Part 7　Incomplete Sentence:
1. C
2. D
3. D
4. B
5. D

Lesson 2

Part 1　Image Listening:
1. B
2. B
3. B
4. B

Part 2　Question and Response: Drills:
1. B
2. A
3. A
4. C
5. A

Part 3　Short Conversation:
1. B
2. A
3. A
4. B

Part 4　Short Talks:
First paragraph:
1. B
2. C
Second paragraph:
1. A
2. D

Part 5　Speed Reading:
First paragraph:
1. D
2. A
Second paragraph:
1. C
2. C
Third paragraph:
1. B
2. C
Comprehension Questions:
1. C
2. A
3. B
4. A

Part 6　Error Recognition:
1. A
2. D
3. D
4. D
5. B
6. D
7. B

Part 7　Incomplete Sentence:
1. A
2. C
3. B
4. B
5. D

Lesson: 3

Part 1　Image Listening:

1. D
2. B
3. D
4. C

Part 2　Question and Response:

Drills:

1. C
2. A
3. C
4. C
5. C

Part 3　Short Conversation:

1. B
2. C
3. A
4. D

Part 4　Short Talks:

First paragraph:

1. B
2. D

Second paragraph:

1. B
2. C

Part 5　Speed Reading:

First paragraph:

1. B
2. D

Second paragraph:

1. B
2. B

Third paragraph:

1. C
2. B

Comprehension Questions:

1. B
2. A
3. B
4. C

Part 6　Error Recognition:

1. C
2. B
3. A
4. A
5. D
6. A
7. C

Part 7　Incomplete Sentence:

1. D
2. D
3. B
4. C
5. A

Lesson: 4

Part 1　Image Listening:

1. D
2. C
3. A
4. B

Part 2　Question and Response:

Drills:

1. C
2. A
3. C
4. C
5. A

Part 3　Short Conversation:

1. C
2. C
3. A
4. D

Part 4　Short Talks:

First paragraph

1. D
2. A

Second paragraph:

1. C
2. B

Part 5　Speed Reading:

First paragraph:

1. A
2. C

Second paragraph:

1. D
2. C

Third paragraph:

1. A
2. C

Comprehension Questions:

1. B
2. C
3. C
4. D

Part 6　Error Recognition:

1. D
2. D
3. B
4. C
5. B
6. C
7. B

Part 7　Incomplete Sentence:

1. B
2. B
3. B
4. C
5. C

Lesson: 5

Part 1　Image Listening:

1. B
2. B
3. B
4. C

Part 2　Question and Response:

Drills:

1. A
2. C
3. B

4. B
5. B

Part 3 Short Conversation:
1. C
2. C
3. C
4. B

Part 4 Short Talks:
First paragraph:
1. B
2. C
Second paragraph:
1. C
2. D

Part 5 Speed Reading:
First paragraph:
1. C
2. B
Second paragraph:
1. D
2. C
Third paragraph:
1. B
2. B
Comprehension Questions:
1. B
2. A
3. C
4. D

Part 6 Error Recognition:
1. A
2. B
3. B
4. A
5. B
6. A
7. B

Part 7 Incomplete Sentence:
1. B

2. B
3. B
4. B
5. C

Lesson: 6
Part 1 Image Listening:
1. C
2. A
3. B
4. D

Part 2 Question and Response:
Drills:
1. A
2. A
3. B
4. B
5. A

Part 3 Short Conversation:
1. B
2. C
3. D
4. B

Part 4 Short Talks:
First paragraph:
1. B
2. C
Second paragraph:
1. C
2. B

Part 5 Speed Reading:
First paragraph:
1. B
2. D
Second paragraph:
1. B
2. A
Third paragraph:
1. D
2. A

Comprehension Questions:
1. C
2. D
3. B
4. A

Part 6 Error Recognition:
1. A
2. C
3. B
4. B
5. A
6. B
7. B

Part 7 Incomplete Sentence:
1. A
2. B
3. A
4. A
5. A

Lesson: 7
Part 1 Image Listening:
1. A
2. D
3. B
4. A

Part 2 Question and Response:
Drills:
1. B
2. A
3. A
4. B
5. B

Part 3 Short Conversation:
1. A
2. B
3. C
4. A

解 答

Part 4　Short Talks:
First paragraph:
1. A
2. C
Second paragraph:
1. A
2. C

Part 5　Speed Reading:
First paragraph:
1. B
2. C
Second paragraph:
1. D
2. B
Third paragraph:
1. D
2. A
Comprehension Questions:
1. A
2. C
3. B
4. C

Part 6　Error Recognition:
1. A
2. A
3. A
4. A
5. C
6. A
7. A

Part 7　Incomplete Sentence:
1. C
2. D
3. B
4. D
5. C

Lesson: 8
Part 1　Image Listening:
1. C
2. B
3. B
4. C

Part 2　Question and Response: Drills:
1. B
2. C
3. C
4. A
5. B

Part 3　Short Conversation:
1. C
2. B
3. C
4. A

Part 4　Short Talks:
First paragraph:
1. B
2. B
Second paragraph:
1. B
2. A

Part 5　Speed Reading:
First paragraph:
1. C
2. A
Second paragraph:
1. C
2. D
Third paragraph:
1. C
2. B
Comprehension Questions:
1. B
2. A
3. D
4. C

Part 6　Error Recognition:
1. A
2. A

3. D
4. A
5. B
6. A
7. C

Part 7　Incomplete Sentence:
1. A
2. C
3. C
4. B
5. D

Lesson: 9
Part 1　Image Listening:
1. C
2. B
3. D
4. A

Part 2　Question and Response: Drills:
1. C
2. C
3. A
4. A
5. A

Part 3　Short Conversation:
1. B
2. D
3. B
4. D

Part 4　Short Talks:
First paragraph:
1. B
2. B
Second paragraph:
1. B
2. C

Part 5 Speed Reading:
First paragraph:
1. A
2. C
Second paragraph:
1. C
2. B
Third paragraph:
1. A
2. D
Comprehension Questions:
1. B
2. C
3. B
4. D

Part 6 Error Recognition:
1. A
2. C
3. B
4. C
5. B
6. C
7. A

Part 7 Incomplete Sentence:
1. C
2. C
3. A
4. C
5. B

Lesson: 10
Part 1 Image Listening:
1. C
2. A
3. B
4. C

Part 2 Question and Response:
Drills:
1. C
2. B
3. B
4. C
5. B

Part 3 Short Conversation:
1. B
2. C
3. A
4. D

Part 4 Short Talks:
First paragraph:
1. B
2. B
Second paragraph:
1. C
2. B

Part 5 Speed Reading:
First paragraph:
1. C
2. D
Second paragraph:
1. D
2. B
Third paragraph:
1. A
2. C
Comprehension Questions:
1. D
2. A
3. D
4. C

Part 6 Error Recognition:
1. C
2. A
3. B
4. A
5. D
6. B
7. B

Part 7 Incomplete Sentence:
1. C
2. D
3. A
4. B
5. D

Lesson: 11
Part 1 Image Listening:
1. B
2. B
3. D
4. A

Part 2 Question and Response:
Drills:
1. B
2. A
3. B
4. A
5. A

Part 3 Short Conversation:
1. C
2. A
3. D
4. D

Part 4 Short Talks:
First paragraph:
1. C
2. D
Second paragraph:
1. C
2. A

Part 5 Speed Reading:
First paragraph:
1. A
2. B
Second paragraph:
1. A
2. C
Third paragraph:
1. C
2. B

Comprehension Questions:

1. B
2. D
3. C
4. B

Part 6　Error Recognition:

1. A
2. C
3. B
4. A
5. C
6. B
7. B

Part 7　Incomplete Sentence:

1. D
2. C
3. B
4. D
5. C

Lesson: 12

Part 1　Image Listening:

1. B
2. C
3. D
4. D

Part 2　Question and Response:

Drills:

1. B
2. A
3. B
4. A
5. A

Part 3　Short Conversation:

1. A
2. B
3. A
4. D

Part 4　Short Talks:

First paragraph:

1. B
2. A

Second paragraph:

1. B
2. A

Part 5　Speed Reading:

First paragraph:

1. A
2. C

Second paragraph:

1. C

2. B

Third paragraph:

1. C
2. D

Comprehension Questions:

1. D
2. D
3. C
4. B

Part 6　Error Recognition:

1. C
2. B
3. D
4. C
5. C
6. D
7. A

Part 7　Incomplete Sentence:

1. D
2. D
3. C
4. B
5. B

■編者紹介

Linc Educational Resources, Inc

　米国大学の英語教育専門家の協力を得ながら、総合メディアによる実用的な英語学習教材の製作に携わっているカリキュラム開発組織。また、短期留学企画・制作、正規留学支援プログラムの運営、アメリカの大学への編入および単位移行もサポートしている。実践的な英語運用能力の開発を支援するための情報収集、オンライン教材開発を主たる活動内容としている。Linc English、Linc Kids（児童、児童英語教育者対象）の執筆・編集を行うとともに、e-ラーニングのシステムの構築、オンライン上での学習管理も行っている。

■監修者・編著者紹介

橘　由加　（たちばな　ゆか）

仙台市出身

東北大学高等教育開発推進センター准教授。

モンタナ大学近代・古典言語文学部准教授（兼任）。

カリフォルニア大学　国際関係学修士課程修了。

東北大学　言語情報学博士課程修了。

　モンタナ大学で日本語学、日米比較文化論、日本文化の准教授として勤務。また、大学内にあるマンスフィールドセンター（国際会議）の通訳も兼ねる。

　2008年度から東北大学高等教育開発推進センターに所属。全学の英語教育推進改革アドバイザーも兼ね、教授陣たちにCALL教授法を指導。東北大学英語部会、学務審議会教員研修委員。

　LINC教材開発顧問。「Linc Englishオンライン・カリキュラムコース」の開発、監修・編著に携わる。

著　書

『アメリカの大学教育の現状』三修社、『大学外国語教育改革』熊本大学文学部文学科（共著）、他。

■Linc Englishについて

　モンタナ大学准教授の橘由加氏を中心に、米国の大学の外国語教育の専門家によって開発された。コンテンツ制作者・文法解説・翻訳者は全員米国の大学でESL/TESOLのトレーニングを受け、言語学、英語学の修士号の資格を持っている。モンタナ大学のコンピュータ・サイエンス、言語学の専門家を中心にチームを編成し、ワシントン大学、カリフォルニア州立大学（ロングビーチ校）、サンフランシスコ州立大学から日米のESL/TESOLの専門家を集め、米国のカリキュラム開発会社Lincによる出資にて、216レッスン、A4判で18,000ページ以上にのぼる莫大なオンライン・コンテンツを、4年を費やし開発した。Linc Englishは音声をとおしてリスニング、読解、文法・語彙力の向上を目指す。また学習・成績管理が容易にでき、英語力がどのように向上しているか管理できるプログラムになっている。忙しい英語教員にとって、学習者の成績管理が容易にでき、採点もしてくれる、という学習管理システムがあるのは非常にありがたいものだろう。Linc Englishはオンライン上で非常に簡単に使え、ユーザーフレンドリーなので、テクノロジーに強くない学習者、教員でも使いこなせることが魅力でもある。費用も経済的な価格で設定されている。個人で購入した場合の1年間の全コースは216レッスンでアクセス費用は39,600円。団体購入の場合、1人当たりの1年間のアクセス費用は受講者数によっても異なるが、6,000円から10,000円前後となる。

［商品に関するお問い合わせ］

Linc Educational Resources, Inc.

666-0145　兵庫県川西市けやき坂1-18-113

ディレクター　笈田美佐

Tel：072-799-3566/mobile：090-7878-5776

URL：www.lincenglish.com　www.lincamerica.com

e-メール：linc_english@jttk.zaq.ne.jp

［商品・本書に関するお問い合わせ］

（株）大学教育出版

700-0953　岡山市西市855-4

URL：www.kyoiku.co.jp

Eメール：info@kyouiku.co.jp

オンライン英語学習用テキスト
Linc English　Bronze II

2009 年 4 月 30 日　初版第 1 刷発行

- ■監修者・編著者────橘　由加
- ■編　　　　　者────Linc Educational Resources, Inc
- ■発　行　者────佐藤　守
- ■発　行　所────株式会社　大学教育出版
  - 〒 700-0953　岡山市西市 855-4
  - 電話（086）244-1268　FAX（086）246-0294
- ■印　刷　製　本────サンコー印刷㈱
- ■装　　　　　丁────ティー・ボーンデザイン事務所

© Yuka Tachibana, Linc Educational Resources, Inc 2009, Printed in Japan
検印省略　　落丁・乱丁本はお取り替えいたします。
無断で本書の一部または全部を複写・複製することは禁じられています。
ISBN978-4-88730-915-9